THE THIRD WAVE
OF THE HOLY SPIRIT

The Third Wave of the Holy Spirit

*Encountering the Power
of Signs and Wonders Today*

C. Peter Wagner

VINE
BOOKS

Servant Publications
Ann Arbor, Michigan

Vine Books is an imprint of Servant Publications especially
designed to serve Evangelical Christians.

Chapters one, two, three, seven, and nine were originally
published as articles in *Christian Life* magazine. Chapters four,
five, six, and eight contain material originally published as
articles in *Ministries Today* magazine and *Christian Life*.

Published by Servant Books
P.O. Box 8617
Ann Arbor, Michigan 48107

Cover design by Steve Eames

90 91 92 10 9 8 7 6 5

Printed in the United States of America
ISBN 0-89283-601-6

Library of Congress Cataloging-in-Publication Data

Wagner, C. Peter
  The third wave of the Holy Spirit : encountering the power
of signs and wonders today / C. Peter Wagner
    p. cm.
  ISBN (invalid) 0-89283-601-6
  1. Holy Spirit. 2. Spiritual healing. 3. Exorcism. 4. Gifts,
Spiritual. 5. Wagner, C. Peter. I. Title.
BT121.2.W28   1988
234'.13—dc19   88-5974
                                                  CIP

Books by C. Peter Wagner

Your Church Can Grow
Your Spiritual Gifts Can Help Your Church Grow
Your Church Can Be Healthy
The Church Growth Survey Handbook
  (with Bob Waymire)
Church Growth and the Whole Gospel
On the Crest of the Wave
Leading Your Church to Growth
Church Growth: State of the Art (editor)
Strategies for Church Growth
Signs and Wonders Today (editor)

Contents

Foreword

WHEN I WAS ASKED TO WRITE this foreword, I thought, "What reasons could I offer for reading *The Third Wave of the Holy Spirit?*" I had little problem coming up with many.

First, I'm enthusiastic about anything written by Peter Wagner, because I'm enthusiastic about Peter Wagner. Over the years I have known him as a man of integrity, a leader who combines scholarship with practical experience. He is my mentor in church growth, but more importantly he is one of my models for Christian living. His character and way of life shine through his writing.

The second reason for reading *The Third Wave of the Holy Spirit* is to learn more about recent trends in worldwide Christianity, trends concerning the ministry of the Holy Spirit and missions that American Christians need to know. Since 1980 I have noticed a dramatic transition in Peter's understanding and experience of the ministry of the Holy Spirit. No, he hasn't moved away from solid evangelical, biblical, and theological convictions, convictions shaped during seminary studies, sixteen years on the mission field, and many years as a faculty member at Fuller Seminary. His feet are firmly planted in biblical orthodoxy, which makes his spiritual transition significant to you and me. In fact, it is his commitment to fulfill the great commission and to see the kingdom of God advance that motivates him to look for solutions to problems in worldwide missions. Much of this book comes from continuing dialogue with seasoned missionaries studying at Fuller's School of World Mission. Peter has discovered one of the keys to missions in the 1980s: a greater understanding and openness to the Holy Spirit, certainly a neglected key for many evangelicals. I have learned much from Peter and I guarantee that you will too.

Third, if you read this book and put it into practice, you will grow spiritually. C. Peter Wagner is a major contributor to missions literature, with more than thirty works published over the past twenty years. But you may not know about his commitment to be a *practitioner* of church growth; when Peter learns something, he puts it into practice—no matter what the cost. That's because he is first and foremost a lover of God. When God tells him to do something, he obeys. This attitude of obedience, not mere intellectual assent, permeates his writing.

Closely related to this is Peter's fierce commitment to an ongoing interaction between orthodoxy (right theology) and orthopraxy (right practice). He is no ivory tower theoretician who makes a living out of criticizing others and never contributing anything positive to the kingdom of God. Peter challenges us to compare what we believe with how we live.

Peter Wagner's consideration and respect for other Christians points to another reason for reading this book: he loves the body of Christ—both individual members and the institutions—and he loves to talk about the good things he sees in the body of Christ. What I find most remarkable is that he loves not only the theory of the church, he loves working out that theory in everyday life. Someone once said that if it weren't for Christians, Christianity would be great; however, all our failures considered, Peter thinks that people trying to love Jesus is what makes Christianity so great! Because he embraces the *whole* body of Christ, his book speaks to all Christian people. You may not agree with everything he writes, but you've got to agree with his spirit of unity and brotherhood.

Finally, Peter writes for practitioners. This work isn't written as a treatise for theologians, though theologians would do well to read and understand what it says. If anything, Peter writes for servants of God, for lay persons, missionaries, and pastors, people who are out in the field putting their lives and reputations on the line daily. This is why I have always loved reading his books: they are on the cutting edge of what God is doing. I highly recommend *The Third Wave of the Holy Spirit* if you want to learn how to fulfill the great commission in our generation.

John Wimber
Yorba Linda, California

Introduction

THE CLOSING YEARS of the twentieth century are seeing a major change in outlook sweeping across traditional Christianity. An increasing number of observers are calling it the "Third Wave."

As I describe in detail in this book, the power of God's Holy Spirit, particularly in the mighty works of New Testament style signs and wonders, has been more prominent in the twentieth century than in any other period of modern church history. The first wave was the Pentecostal movement, the second the charismatic movement, and now the third wave is joining them. Researcher David Barrett estimates that the first two waves numbered some 247 million as of 1987 and the third wave 27 million.

I believe that the major change in our traditional churches will be a dramatic increase in the ministry of healing the sick. I would not be surprised if, before the year 2000, the majority of churches in a community will be carrying on an overt, up front, active and effective healing ministry. They, of course, will not replace medical science and other healing professionals. But more and more sick people will consider looking to their churches as well as to doctors and hospitals for healing.

This book is highly personal. In it I tell how I myself, being a very traditional evangelical Christian, moved into a ministry of praying for the sick and helping others do it in ways somewhat different from the first two waves. Not that I want to pour others into my mold, but I do want to communicate clearly something of a major contemporary movement of God.

This book will help you and your church to see what God is doing here in the United States and around the world; it will allow you to interpret these sometimes dramatic activities in the light of the Bible and Christian tradition; it will put you in touch with an often neglected dimension of the supernatural; and it will guide you as you seek to allow the power of God to be channelled through you for the blessing of many.

ONE

How I Learned about the Power

F OR SOME YEARS NOW THE HOLY SPIRIT has begun to work in a way that is somewhat different or even strange to many of us evangelicals. I first became aware of this work as an observer. More recently I have become a participator. I now see it as something extremely important for all believers in Christ. While such a judgment always is highly suspect, I even go so far as to predict that this new movement of the Holy Spirit will have historical significance.

The label "Third Wave" surfaced while I was being interviewed on this subject by *Pastoral Renewal* magazine. So far as I can tell, it has no relationship to the title of Alvin Toffler's best-selling book, *The Third Wave*. It is simply a term which I found convenient at the moment, and which some others now have picked up, to describe this new activity of the Holy Spirit.

"Third Wave" implies two previous waves, and this is how I perceive the Holy Spirit working in the twentieth century.

The first wave was known as the Pentecostal movement. It began in the United States at the turn of the century and soon spread to other parts of the world. The major characteristic of the Pentecostal movement was a powerful ministry of the Holy Spirit in the realm of the miraculous that most other Christians at the time found highly unusual.

Prominent among the miraculous works were what have been called baptism in the Holy Spirit, speaking in tongues, healing the sick, and casting out demons. It also brought with it an openness and freedom to public worship which at times involved a rather high noise level, praying with upraised hands, emotional demonstrations, falling on the floor, and even some dancing in the Spirit.

The majority of Christians were not prepared for this outpouring of the Holy Spirit. For one thing, they had no theology for handling it. For many, the miraculous signs and wonders that we read about in the New Testament were restricted to that period of history. Many prestigious theologians and Bible teachers were arguing that the sign gifts such as tongues, healing, miracles, and discernment of spirits were needed only until the New Testament canon had been established.

Because there was no theological grid for understanding what the Holy Spirit was doing through the Pentecostal movement, many evangelicals did the only thing they knew how: They declared Pentecostals heretics. In some of the older books on the false cults you will see Pentecostals listed alongside Jehovah's Witnesses, Mormons, and Christian Scientists.

Evangelicals also had a difficult time relating to the Pentecostals emotionally. Especially in the eyes of those coming from the more sedate denominations, what the Pentecostals were doing in their churches was not Christianity at all. A few went so far as to attribute the Pentecostal manifestations to the devil himself. Some labeled them "holy rollers."

It took the classical Pentecostals almost half a century to gain respectability among other Protestants. But leaders such as David du Plessis among the ecumenicals and Thomas Zimmerman among the evangelicals helped turn the tide. Many Pentecostal groups are members of the National Association of Evangelicals and they cooperate broadly with interdenominational activities.

The second major wave of the Holy Spirit in the twentieth century was the charismatic movement emerging around the middle of the century. This was the beginning of the fulfillment of the dream of the early Pentecostal leaders that the miraculous power of the Holy Spirit would be introduced into the mainline denominations. The charismatic movement has been strong in the Catholic Church as well as in such Protestant denominations as Episcopal, Lutheran, Presbyterian, United Methodist, and many others.

Ironically, when the charismatic movement took root it usually brought with it a more evangelical way of looking at Scriptures and of understanding conversion and the new birth. Even so, most evangelicals could not welcome the movement because their conservative theology was not able to accept the miraculous as a valid part of today's Christian experience. Frequently when members of evangelical churches received the charismatic experience they were either forced out of their churches or the churches split.

The major symbolic point of rejection of charismatics among evangelicals was baptism in the Holy Spirit and speaking in tongues.

The Third Wave is a new moving of the Holy Spirit among evangelicals who, for one reason or another, have chosen not to identify with either the Pentecostals or the charismatics. Its roots go back a little further, but I see it as mainly a movement beginning in the 1980s and gathering momentum through the closing years of the twentieth century. Researcher David Barrett estimates 27 million third-wavers in 1988. In it the Holy Spirit is ministering in the same miraculous way but with a different flavor. I see the Third Wave as distinct from, but at the same time very similar to the first and second waves. They have to be similar because it is the same Spirit of God who is doing the work.

The major distinguishing point of the Third Wave is not the final result of the ministry of the Holy Spirit. Within it the sick are being healed, the lame are walking, demons are being cast out, and other New Testament manifestations of supernatural power are seen. This has been happening among Pentecostals and charismatics for years.

The major variation comes in the understanding of the meaning of baptism in the Holy Spirit and the role of tongues in authenticating this. I myself, for example, would rather not have people call me a charismatic. I do not consider myself a charismatic. I am simply an evangelical Congregationalist who is open to the Holy Spirit working through me and my church in any way he chooses.

A Missionary without Power

Like the Apostle Paul, I committed my life to missionary service at the time of my conversion. I was nineteen. From that point on I was sold out to obeying Jesus' great commission to "make disciples of all nations." I served sixteen years as a missionary to Bolivia and I am now in my seventeenth year as a professor of missions here in the United States.

Through the years I have familiarized myself with the biblical appearances of the great commission. It is found in each of the four Gospels and in the Book of Acts. I have read and reread them. In fact my personalized automobile license plate is "Mt 28:19" and my wife's is "Mt 28:20," so wherever we go, we go with the great commission.

As I look back now from the perspective I have developed during the last two or three years, I am amazed—amazed at what I did not see as I previously read those verses. I now realize that every one is accompanied by a clear power promise.

Let's take a look.

In Matthew 28, before Jesus says "Go and make disciples of all nations," he says "All power is given to me" (v. 18). In Mark 16:17 Jesus commands his disciples to preach the gospel to every creature. Then he says,

"And these signs shall follow those who believe." In Luke 24, Jesus tells his disciples that they will be witnesses of the things they have seen. But first they must "tarry in the city of Jerusalem until you are endued with power from on high" (v. 49). In John 20 Jesus says to his disciples, "As the Father has sent me, I also send you," followed immediately by, "Receive the Holy Spirit" (vv. 21-22). In Acts 1:8, he tells them that before they become his witnesses they will receive power when the Holy Spirit has come upon them.

The Bible, therefore, is clear that divine power is to accompany the spread of the gospel. But what is that power for? What kind of power is it?

Previously, I thought it was power for witnessing and for living a godly life. And I still think it is. But an important dimension of that power had eluded me completely. It is the power that Jesus gave to his twelve disciples the first time he sent them out on their own: "He gave them power over unclean spirits to cast them out, and to heal all kinds of sickness and all kinds of disease" (Mt 10:1). That word for power is *exousia*, which also appears in the great commission of Matthew 28, "All power is given me."

To my surprise, as I look back on the sixteen years I served as a missionary in the Third World I cannot recall that kind of power ever operating in my ministry. I never cast out an evil spirit. I never healed a sick person. I did pray for sick people from time to time, usually the "Heal this person if it be your will" type of prayer. But so far as I know the power to *heal* the sick, which I frequently see now, was not there.

How could this be? I was a Bible-believing evangelical Christian minister with at least an average level of maturity and spirituality. But the more I think about it, the more I am convinced that my lack of contact with supernatural power was due to the pervasive influences of secular humanism through all levels of our contemporary American culture. It is not only in our public schools and universities, but it is in our churches, Bible schools, and seminaries.

I was taught in seminary that while the apostles healed the sick and cast out demons as part of their regular ministry, we in our present sophisticated age were not supposed to do that. I was taught that now that we had the Word of God in Scripture, the miraculous power in the ministry of the first century no longer was needed.

A recent research project turned up the fact that of 87,000 pages of theological reference works in the library of a prominent evangelical seminary, only 288 touched on divine power. That is about one third of one percent. No wonder entire generations of ministers go out relatively powerless.

This secular humanism, I am ashamed to admit, actually caused me to be a secularizing force when I went to Bolivia. For example, I always had been taught the "germ theory" of disease. When I got to Bolivia I came upon some folks who, while they believed many diseases were caused by germs, also thought that some diseases were caused by evil spirits.

My reaction? I pitied them.

"It's too bad these poor people are so superstitious," I said. My assumption was that if they accepted Christ and became evangelical Christians, they soon would get rid of that nonsense. Christians believe in germs, not spirits, I thought. God cures diseases, but nowadays it is with injections, capsules, and operations, not with oil on the forehead.

Then the Pentecostal faith healers would come to town and put up their tents. I would become furious, and write articles accusing them of fraud. I would tell the people in my church not to go to their meetings. (Later I learned that they went anyhow.)

A Missionary Converted

What brought about the change? How did I turn 180 degrees?

The process took about fifteen years. First, in the later sixties, I had an unforgettable experience. I attended a meeting to hear E. Stanley Jones, the famous Methodist missionary to India. It turned out to be an old-fashioned healing service, and I was miraculously healed of a runny sore on my neck which was scheduled for surgery the following week. For the first time, a crack began to appear in my previous theories.

About the same time, I began studying church growth under my mentor, Donald McGavran. He taught me to be relentless about discovering where churches were growing vigorously and why God was blessing them. No sooner did I develop "church growth eyes" than I began to be aware of the tremendous surge in the Pentecostal movement in Latin America, especially in Chile. So I traveled there from time to time and looked in on the Pentecostals.

The church I visited most was the Jotabeche Methodist Pentecostal Church, at that time the largest church in the world. As I heard the preaching of Pastor Javier Vasquez and felt the presence of the Holy Spirit in the boisterous worship services, I realized this was no fraud. I began to wonder if perhaps it wasn't more like New Testament Christianity than some of the churches with which I was associated. I mentioned all this in a book I wrote in the early seventies now called *Spiritual Power and Church Growth,* but for many years I remained an interested spectator rather than a participant.

By then I was back in the States, and God began to open doors of ministry among Pentecostals—Assemblies of God, Pentecostal Holiness, and especially Church of God (Cleveland, Tennessee)—here at home. In some Church of God meetings I was ministered to more than ministering.

All this prepared me for getting to know John Wimber, whom God used to make me a participant rather than a spectator. When John and I first became associated in ministry in the mid-seventies, neither of us knew anything about experiencing the miraculous power of God. Then Wimber became the founding pastor of Vineyard Christian Fellowship which began in his living room and soon grew to a church of over 6,000.

Before long, the *exousia* power of Matthew 10:1, which I mentioned earlier, was in full operation. The sick were being healed (not just prayed for) and demons were being cast out. God began doing signs and wonders through John Wimber and the people in his church that I previously had thought could be done only through Pentecostals.

Because I trusted John, I never doubted that what was happening at Vineyard Christian Fellowship was authentic New Testament Christianity. The upshot: I teamed up with John to offer a new course in Fuller Seminary, MC510, first called "Signs, Wonders and Church Growth," later renamed "The Miraculous and Church Growth."

The course began in January 1982. It was there I began to see, right in the seminary classroom, what happens when the power of God is unleashed. Night after night I saw words of knowledge verified on the spot, sick people instantly healed, evil spirits cast out, and many other manifestations of supernatural ministry.

Before the quarter was over, I had become a participant. My ministry, as well as the ministry of hundreds of others, had been revolutionized. I am still a beginner, but I am learning.

TWO

The Power in the Seminary

"**I** KNOW OF ONLY TWO SEMINARY COURSES which have become famous," said Robert Meye, Dean of the Fuller Seminary School of Theology, at a joint faculty meeting. "One was the course on dogmatics taught at Basel by Karl Barth and the other is MC510 taught by John Wimber here at Fuller."

It is true that the general public knows very little about the content of courses taught in seminaries and Bible schools. The major reason MC510 has been an exception is due to the special interest Robert Walker, editor of *Christian Life*, took in it. He made a special fact-finding trip to California in early 1982, then used virtually the whole October 1982 issue of *Christian Life* to report MC510, then called "Signs, Wonders, and Church Growth." It quickly became known as "the sold out issue," and was reprinted in the popular book, *Signs & Wonders Today*, currently being used as a study guide in churches and other Christian groups across the country.

Because of this and the subsequent publicity given the course by the Christian media, MC510 made Fuller Seminary somewhat controversial. For example, I have heard some say that "Fuller Seminary is going charismatic." Those who make that statement are not aware that MC510 was only one course of many hundreds taught there, or that the students who took it are only a handful among the some 2,800 enrolled in its three schools. They also do not realize that a number of respected Fuller faculty members were not altogether happy that the course was being taught. These professors disagree with a theology which argues that signs, wonders, and miracles as seen in the ministry of Jesus and the apostles are to be expected in today's church. As a result the MC510 course was discontinued after four years and a new course, MC550 "The Ministry of Healing in World Evangelization" substituted for it.

No, Fuller is not a charismatic seminary. It is simply evangelical and multi-denominational. Thus, it is neither Baptist nor Presbyterian, Calvinistic nor Wesleyan, pretrib nor post-trib, charismatic nor noncharismatic. People representing all those options—and many others—teach and study there. The intent of the seminary is to avoid extremism in any Christian position, and to strike a biblical balance by allowing all sides of given issues to be presented. As seminary president David Allan Hubbard says, "Hazarding the risks of this approach to the life of the Spirit is part of what Fuller is prepared to do."

Comments such as "Fuller is becoming charismatic,"

therefore, are superficial. But not so all the comments and criticisms of MC510. Many are more substantial, based on first-hand observation, participation, and careful analysis. But before I share some of them, let me review how the course came about.

What Happened in MC510

A key part of my own spiritual pilgrimage was my close friendship with John Wimber, which began in the mid-1970s. At that time he became an adjunct professor in the church growth program.

In 1981, John suggested that he present to a class of doctoral students a new lecture on the relationship of signs and wonders to church growth. I agreed. It went so well that our School of World Mission invited John to try an experimental course (MC510) on the subject in 1982. It was taught five times to overflowing classrooms.

What was the course like?

It was taught on ten successive Monday nights throughout the quarter. For three hours John Wimber lectured on topics such as the relationship of program evangelism to power evangelism, the kingdom of God, biblical records of the miraculous, worldviews, case studies of the miraculous, spiritual gifts, contemporary faith healers, and many others.

The lectures were enlivened with vivid personal illustrations from John's own experience. Free questioning and discussion was encouraged.

Following the lecture was an hour or so of "hands on"

ministry time. There was no predetermined format for this. John opened himself to the direction of the Holy Spirit, and received divine cues in leading it. Sometimes it began with words of knowledge from John. Sometimes members of the class had words of knowledge. Sometimes class members who needed prayer would come up front and John would describe, in a clinical way, just what God was doing to them through the prayer. Sometimes many prayer groups would form spontaneously throughout the classroom. Sometimes it was quiet, sometimes quite noisy.

But every time, without an exception which I can recall, God was pleased to show his power in a tangible way. Many were healed physically. Many received spiritual or emotional healing. Some were filled with the Holy Spirit. Some, for the first time, laid hands on, prayed for a sick person, and saw him or her healed. Some shook under the anointing of the Holy Spirit. Some rested in the Spirit.

This combination of cognitive input and firsthand experience was life-changing for many of the students. Some, of course, came to MC510 with a background which had oriented them to the supernatural. Of those who arrived either neutral or skeptical, well over 90 percent left the classroom convinced that God's power is for today. A good number of them began ministering in the power of the Spirit immediately.

My friend George Eckart is an example. When George enrolled in the course in the winter of 1982, he was asking, "Can I, a Baptist, be used by God to heal the sick?" It was an honest question. Nothing in his background had provided an answer. But after three weeks, George began praying for the sick. A close friend was healed of a knee problem. Another who had been experiencing years of pain from a back injury was freed from the pain. He saw emotional healing, spiritual healing, and the empowerment of the Holy Spirit. Now George is a member of my Sunday School class, the 120 Fellowship, and the leader of a prayer team that regularly is used by God to heal the sick and cast out demons. He has begun offering healing seminars for others who desire this kind of ministry.

Canadian psychiatrist Dr. John White and his wife Lorrie took a three month leave, moved to Pasadena, and enrolled in MC510 in the winter of 1984.

"I had discovered I was trapped within what has been called a Western mind-set, a cultural bias that impeded my capacity to perceive the supernatural phenomena," John explains. "I believed that not only were demonic manifestations commoner than most evangelical Christians suppose, but that the Holy Spirit was at work in miraculous ways among the people of God. I also believed the kind of manifestations common in the Gospels and in the Acts should not be regarded as terminating with the death of the apostles or the completion of the scriptural canon, but should be regarded as normative."

He was positively impressed by MC510, and since has helped many others to be open to the power of God.

People like John White are key figures in what I am calling the "Third Wave," the contemporary movement of the Holy Spirit among traditional evangelicals. The

"Western mind-set" John White talks about undoubtedly is a chief barrier to many of us being open to the work of the supernatural in daily life.

The Excluded Middle

I spent sixteen years, almost half of my ministry to date, as a missionary. Now, at Fuller Seminary, I am part of the largest missiological faculty in the world, with twelve full-time (and several part-time) professors. The twelve of us have many things in common, but one of them we discovered only recently: during our overseas missionary careers we (with one exception) were almost totally blind to what we now know as the "middle zone." We have come to realize—first to our surprise, then to our regret—that a significant effect of our ministry in the Third World might have been a secularizing one.

Our question now is: How could we have gone with a message we presumed would help bring people in touch with the supernatural, when in some cases we were ignoring important aspects of the supernatural?

I do not mean to imply that God did not bless our ministry. Souls were saved, churches planted, lives transformed, people called into full-time ministry, Scriptures translated, pastors trained, schools and hospitals built, indigenous literature produced, and any number of other good results of missionary work.

It took one of our number, Paul G. Hiebert, to alert us to a serious defect in otherwise sound missionary strategy. He wrote an article in 1982 called "The Flaw of the Excluded Middle." He begins by quoting the question that John the Baptist's disciples asked Jesus: "Are you he that should come or do we look for another?" (Lk 7:20). Jesus' response, he points out, was not some carefully reasoned argument but a demonstration of power in curing the sick and casting out evil spirits.

Hiebert, who is professor of anthropology, religions, and South Asian studies, continues by giving his own personal experience. He says, "Yet when I read the passage as a missionary in India and sought to apply it to missions in our day, I had a sense of uneasiness. As a Westerner, I was used to presenting Christ on the basis of rational arguments, not by evidence of his power in the lives of people who were sick, possessed and destitute. In particular," Hiebert says, "the confrontation with spirits that appeared so natural a part of Christ's ministry belonged in my mind to a separate world of the miraculous—far from ordinary everyday experience."

He goes on to point out that the worldview of most non-Westerners is three-tiered. The top tier is high religion based on cosmic personalities or forces. It is very distant. The bottom tier is everyday life: marriages, raising children, planting crops, rain and drought, sickness and health, and what have you. The middle zone includes the normal way these everyday phenomena are influenced by superhuman and supernatural forces. There is no question in their minds that every day they are influenced by spirits, demons, ancestors, goblins, ghosts, magic, fetishes, witches, mediums, sorcerers, and any number of other powers.

This seems strange to many Western missionaries when they arrive in such cultures. I have before me a prayer letter from Elsa Korbonen, a Wycliffe missionary to Ethiopia studying the Haddiya language. She reports: "The churches are crowded, but many of the Christians are involved in some sort of witchcraft, or are very much under fear of the spirits. Witchcraft is practiced in the area, and witches are cursing and binding people. It is common to have prayer meetings (often in the church after the service) where the demon possessed are freed and sick people are healed."

Such experience is rare in the United States evangelical churches because most of us who have been born or educated in the West have been programmed with a two-tiered worldview. We are able to handle a top tier of cosmic religion, and we pretty well confine the supernatural to that zone. We are very comfortable with a bottom tier which is governed by science. Whatever happens in our everyday life usually is explained by some scientific cause-and-effect relationship. When we run up against something we can't explain, we generally feel that given the rapid advance of science, it will eventually be discovered.

The middle zone? It is absent. We feel that those who take it seriously are "superstitious," and that our task is to enlighten them so that they will be more scientific and less gullible.

A clear example of this was published recently in *Christianity Today* in an article called "A Surgeon's View of Divine Healing." The surgeon who writes it is a committed Christian who has accumulated forty years of experience in the medical field. He admits to having mixed emotions about current enthusiasm over faith healing.

"Although I share the same goals as the faith healers I see on television, in techniques and style we differ enormously," he says. He could have added they also differ in worldview. His typical Western two-tiered worldview is expressed like this: "I believe in the divine component of healing. But my own contributions to patients come after years of study and the application of rigid scientific principles to laws governing human physiology." He tells how it may take two or three years of a series of surgeries and rehabilitation to restore a leprosy patient's deformed hand.

"And yet," he says, "some faith healers seem to promise an entirely new kind of medicine, an instantaneous healing that defies the normal process of science."

Those of us whom God has caught up in the Third Wave can hear what this surgeon says clearly because most of us at one time shared his worldview. We excluded the middle so categorically that in many cases we found ourselves ministering out there on the mission field with "one hand tied behind our backs," as my colleague, Dean Gilliland, so aptly puts it. He tells how a Nigerian pastor whose wife was demonized came to him for help. When Gilliland admitted to him that he did not know how to release God's power in this middle zone area of ministry, the poor Nigerian pastor took his wife to a pagan exorcist to have her delivered.

Healing the sick and casting out demons? Another of our faculty members, Charles Kraft, points out that most of us were taught that such activity ended in the first century. Then, he says, we go to the mission field. "There we find that, very often, God is doing these things. Dreams, healing, demon possession, all are experienced. So," says Kraft, "to keep our belief system intact, we explain away all these things. Soon the people just stop telling us about the happenings. They know we aren't open to them."

There are three billion people in the world yet to believe in Jesus Christ. An overwhelming majority of them have a three-tiered worldview. The middle zone is very real to them, as it is throughout the New Testament. Their worldview is, in that respect, more biblical than most of ours. What happens, then, when we go out to them with our scientific programming? We simply don't communicate.

"So long as the missionary comes with a two-tier worldview operating for all practical purposes according to autonomous scientific laws, Christianity will continue to be a secularizing force in the world," Paul Hiebert says.

The surgeon I mentioned previously writes, "Not once have I seen a missing finger suddenly grow back." Chances are he never expected it to. But a short time after I read that article, my friend John Wimber phoned me to report on a healing seminar he had just conducted in Seattle. With several physicians present, a woman's toe, which had been cut off, completely grew back, toenail and all. John's worldview has not excluded the middle.

As we train missionaries at the Fuller School of World Mission, we are becoming increasingly aware of the need to address the middle zone. Our dean, Paul Pierson, recently returned from a trip to Brazil where he previously served as a missionary. He reported that there are 80 million practicing spiritists in that one nation. He told how on a certain evening more than 300,000 people from one city gathered on the beach to make sacrifices to the goddess of the sea.

"What I learned in Princeton Seminary," he said, "did not prepare me to deal with this phenomenon."

When Jesus gave the great commission, he said, "All power is given to me. Go you therefore and make disciples of all nations ... and I will be with you always."

I am intensely interested in learning more about that power so I can share it with others.

THREE

Faith for Power

M OST CHRISTIANS FEEL THEY SHOULD have more faith. But that goal is somewhat elusive because it is so vague. My hope is to dispel the fog of generalities which we usually attach to faith so that we can understand more concretely what it means for us.

As a starting point, let's think of Biblical faith as including four facets. In some way, there is a progression from one to the other. However, with the exception of the first facet, the four do not necessarily build on each other in the sense that one needs to have achieved near perfection in one facet in order to proceed to the next. No. Elements of all can be going on at the same time in your life, and you can be growing in each facet.

The first facet is *saving faith*. This is basic, and it is a prerequisite to all other facets. You can't be a Christian without saving faith. Believing in Jesus as Savior and Lord restores the fellowship with the Father which Adam lost in the Garden of Eden. "For God so loved the world that he gave his only begotten Son, that whosoever believes (has faith!) on him should not perish but have everlasting life" (Jn 3:16). When we talk about missionaries going out into the world to "spread the faith," this is the faith to which we are referring.

The second facet is *sanctifying faith*. This faith is a fruit of the Spirit. Once we have saving faith and become followers of Jesus, the Holy Spirit comes into our lives. We grow in grace. The indwelling of the Holy Spirit always manifests himself in good works. That's why faith without works is dead. Life in the Holy Spirit is life in his fruits: love, joy, peace, patience, longsuffering, gentleness, goodness, faith. . . . (Gal 5:22-23). Whereas there are no degrees of saving faith—either you are saved or you are not—there are degrees of sanctifying faith. Babes in Christ have all the saving faith they need, but very little sanctifying faith. The Christian life is a continuous challenge to develop more sanctifying faith and thereby live a more godly life and be a better witness for Jesus Christ.

For most of my Christian experience these two were the only facets of faith I knew anything about. The evangelical preaching to which I was exposed did a good job of sensitizing me to saving faith and sanctifying faith. But it did not take me much further.

The third facet of faith I like to call *possibility-thinking faith*. The name comes from the title of a book by Pastor Robert Schuller, *Move Ahead with Possibility Thinking*. Schuller has helped many people begin to believe God for great things. This is faith for setting goals. A somewhat mysterious but important dynamic is released through intelligent and courageous goal setting.

Hebrews 11 is a textbook on possibility-thinking

faith. It begins by defining faith as "the substance of things hoped for." Notice that things hoped for are neither past nor present. Everything hoped for is future. So when we look into the future and put substance on what we see there, we exercise this kind of faith. That is exactly what is involved in goal setting. Later, this chapter in Hebrews says, "Without faith it is impossible to please him" (11:6). This is setting goals and believing God for reaching them. Illustrations abound. Abraham did it when he left Ur of the Chaldees. Noah did it when he built a huge ark on dry ground. It is the faith that "subdued kingdoms, worked righteousness, obtained promises, and stopped the mouth of lions" (Heb 11:33).

As I have studied church growth through the years, I have discovered that as a rule pastors of growing churches are possibility thinkers. They have faith that God is going to move powerfully through their ministry, and he does. Because of this, I have learned to challenge pastors of plateaued or declining churches to set significant goals as one means of overcoming non-growth.

In many cases it works. I am thinking of one church here in Southern California which was declining so severely over several years that the church officers had made the official decision to close down. Then they learned church growth principles and set goals. They soon called a pastor who practiced possibility-thinking faith. Five years later they were over 500 in membership and over 1,000 in attendance.

The fourth facet of faith is *fourth-dimension faith*. Again, I have taken it from a book title, this time from *The Fourth Dimension*, by Paul Yonggi Cho. Cho is pastor of Yoido Full Gospel Church in Seoul, Korea, the world's largest church. The membership has surpassed 500,000. Cho understands and practices the first three levels of faith, but he adds another. He believes God for supernatural signs and wonders. He sees God do miraculous things as a part of his everyday ministry.

Fourth-dimension faith is described in the Bible in Matthew 17. Jesus' disciples came across an epileptic who had a demon. They tried to heal him but couldn't. Then Jesus cast out the demon and used the opportunity to teach a lesson. When the disciples asked why they couldn't cast out the demon, Jesus said, "Because of your unbelief!" (Mt 17:20). He said that faith no larger than a mustard seed would have been sufficient.

What kind of faith was Jesus referring to? His disciples already had saving faith, and a good degree of sanctifying faith. Whether they had possibility-thinking faith I do not know. But they did not, at that time, have the fourth-dimension faith necessary to see a miracle happen. Later on they did demonstrate that faith, particularly after Pentecost. The Book of Acts tells us that many signs and wonders were done through the apostles (Acts 2:43).

Fourth-dimension faith is called the "shield of faith" as part of the full armor of God described in Ephesians 6. This is the faith which can withstand the attacks of principalities and powers and rulers of the darkness of this age. It is the only effective weapon we have in the ongoing battle with Satan and his angels.

This fourth facet of faith is perhaps the most characteristic element of the movement we are calling the "Third Wave." Most of us who have been nurtured in our Christian experience through mainstream evangelicalism have been taught little or nothing about fourth-dimension faith. We pray for the sick with little expectation that the person will get well. We see so few miracles of the Holy Spirit in our lives that we develop theological reasons why we should not expect God to do such things in this particular age.

We have enough faith to believe that Jesus and his disciples did miracles, but when we hear reports of dead people being raised or the blind seeing or the paralyzed walking today we tend to say, "Let me see the X-rays." Even though 1 Corinthians 13:7 says, "Love believes all things," our frequent reaction is skepticism rather than belief. I can hear Jesus saying, "O, ye of little faith."

I see this unbelief in the fourth facet of faith undergoing a change in our day, however. Reports come in with increasing frequency of God moving in his supernatural power through those of us identified with traditional evangelicalism. Some of these experiences have been truly spectacular.

Defeating the Witch Doctor

Adi Sutanto, an Indonesian Christian leader, was a student of mine in the Fuller School of World Mission.

In 1977 he started Sankakala Mission in his homeland. One major feature of this ministry is power evangelism. He and his associates expect God to work through them with mighty miracles, and he does.

Why? Sutanto first gives biblical reasons. He argues that performing signs and wonders in the power of the Holy Spirit "is not just a method, but is an essential part of the coming of the Kingdom of God itself." Power evangelism "is not optional but a necessity," he says. "In other words, this is the normal way the gospel should be preached."

He also gives many practical reasons why their experience in planting churches in Indonesia forces them to lean heavily on the power of God.

"In ministry, especially among the animistic peoples of Java, we often face challenges where the only way to win is to demonstrate the power of God," he says.

Sutanto tells of one of his friends, Pak A, a church planter who went into the jungle area of Central Sulawesi to plant churches.

When Pak A entered a certain village to share the gospel he found himself face to face with a powerful witch doctor, known throughout the area. The witch doctor was determined to stop the spread of the gospel on the spot. With the village people looking on, he pointed his fingers to a calendar which was hanging on a wall about ten feet away. Then he challenged Pak A.

"Watch the power of my gods," he cried, "then show me what your God can do!" With that the calendar was instantly torn apart.

Pak A was shocked. But fortunately he had risen to what I call the "fourth level of faith." He was tuned in to the miraculous power of God in signs and wonders. He opened his heart to the Holy Spirit, and received instructions directly from God. He spoke gently but firmly to the witch doctor and those gathered around.

"The evil spirits always tear things apart and destroy them," he declared. "But the good God came to correct them and help us."

With that he pointed his finger at the torn calendar and a miracle happened. Instantly the calendar was put back the way it was!

No wonder Pak A continued successfully to plant churches in Central Sulawesi.

Many Americans have a difficult time relating to incidents like this. They say, "That may be all right for Indonesia where people are victims of paganism and superstition. But it has no place in a modern, enlightened, scientific country like ours."

This kind of thinking plays right into the devil's hands. There has never been a time when the power of the enemy has not been strong in the United States, but many observers believe it has been intensifying in recent years. The emergence of what some call the "New Age Movement" may well be a chief manifestation of new, subtle forces of evil. How can we confront such forces if not through the direct, immediate, tangible power of God?

Victory in California

Closer to home, another student of mine, Lisa Tunstall, along with her husband John, is planting a new church in Inglewood, California, called The

Abundant Life Christian Church. She arrived late to class one day because John had received an emergency 1:30 A.M. call to the home of a parishioner. When the call came, he could hear strange voices in the background. And the woman speaking was in near panic.

Entering the house, he saw a small group gathered around a woman who belonged to his church. Slouched in a chair, she stared at him with a weird look in her eyes. A masculine voice came from her mouth and said very slowly, "You are the man of God? I have been waiting for you. Show me your power."

John Tunstall is a minister of the Disciples of Christ, a denomination which does not currently specialize in power evangelism. But he and Lisa have been part of the Third Wave, and for some time have known how to minister in the power of the Holy Spirit. He knew he was face to face with an evil spirit, so he replied, "Show me *your* power."

Against the wall was a board shelf resting on cinder blocks and holding a potted plant. Instantly the board cracked and the flower pot blew to pieces with a loud noise.

But John was ready for it. He said, "My power is the blood of the Lord Jesus Christ. In Jesus' name I command you to leave that woman."

The evil spirit struggled before it left. The woman slithered out of the chair onto the floor just like a snake, then writhed around. But before long the power of Jesus prevailed, the demon left, and the woman was completely well.

Little wonder that in less than one year the Tunstalls' congregation was approaching 500.

Whether in Indonesia or Inglewood, the power of Satan is real. But it need not be feared because the power of God is so much greater. I believe the reason we do not see more such power encounters is largely because of our lack of faith in the power of God. We fear we may be victims of our own presumption or audacity. And this, of course, could happen. All the more reason we must learn how to get in touch with the Holy Spirit to know in a more direct and certain way how he wants to use us at a given moment.

How many of us God wants to use in visible, direct confrontations with the principalities and powers I do not know. I myself have never been engaged in a deliberate power encounter, at least one that I know of. I might have been in some and lost because, for one thing, I was too naive to realize what was going on; for another, I had not been informed or trained as to how to tap into the power of God in such a situation.

This is one reason I feel it is so important to begin to get in touch with the power of God these days. This is why we teach it at Fuller Seminary. This is why I teach it in my Sunday School class.

A good deal of effective evangelism has been done through rational, logical presentations of the Word of God. We need to continue and increase what is being called "program evangelism." But over and above this we need to engage in "power evangelism," for there are certain situations in which logic simply will not prevail.

The Apostle Paul encountered a situation like that when he arrived to plant a church in Corinth. He said that when he went there he did not go "with skillful words of human wisdom," which he was quite capable of doing. Rather, he went with "convincing proof of the power of God's Spirit" (2:4 GNB). He reminded them that "the Kingdom of God is not a matter of words, but of power" (1 Cor 4:20).

As we become more accustomed to ministering like the Apostle Paul, and like Adi Sutanto and Pak A, and like John and Lisa Tunstall, the possibility of fulfilling the great commission in our generation becomes more of a reality.

FOUR

A Model for Ministry

I T IS ONE THING TO THEORIZE and write about the Third Wave or to hear about spectacular examples from others. It is something else to experience it firsthand. A significant part of my own experience has been emerging from an adult Sunday School class I helped start in 1982 at my church, Lake Avenue Congregational Church of Pasadena, California. Called "The 120 Fellowship," the class is named after the group which had gathered together in the upper room on the day of Pentecost.

The class got off to a good start with 88 in attendance. I thought many of them would be curiosity seekers and that the attendance would drop. But it held its own for a year, then grew to a total of around 100 adults.

In the beginning no one had intended the class to become anything different from the many other adult classes in the church. The adult Sunday School program, under the direction of Ray Syrstad, Pastor of Lay Ministries, is extremely strong. Some 60-70 percent of adults who attend the worship service also attend a Sunday School class. Because the church is so large

(4,500 members, 3,000 attendance), such classes are essential if meaningful fellowship is to take its normal place on a personal level. In the Sunday School class you know and you are known.

From the outset we began studying the Book of Acts. My intention was to breeze through that book fairly rapidly and get on to some others. But the unexpected happened. We soon realized that the 120 Fellowship was not only *studying* the Book of Acts, but was also beginning to *live it*. This caused me to slow down the pace of the teaching and to stress depth rather than breadth. As I did, we discovered that the power of the Holy Spirit began to manifest itself in unusual ways in the class. Sick people were healed. Demons were cast out. The poor were cared for. Miraculous answers to prayer were reported on a regular basis. The 120 Fellowship had become part of the Third Wave!

A key to the growth of the class was a group of strongly gifted and motivated people whom God gave to the class early on. They had a deep desire to be "doers of the Word," not just hearers. Many of them had not been active in an adult Sunday School class prior to that time. Some came from other classes. As the news of the power of God spread, some even transferred their membership from other churches where they felt they were not being adequately fed or where they felt they were not allowed to minister freely. God gave us people with gifts of administration, service, helps, mercy, healing, exorcism, prophecy, exhortation, pastoring, discerning of spirits, intercession, giving, and many others.

I find that I desperately need all these people and all these gifts. I am a full-time seminary professor and attempt to maintain a national and international speaking ministry. I am not on the staff of my church; my status there is no different from that of any other lay person. I am committed to my church, but the time I can spend in ministry there is quite limited. This is why I enjoy sitting back and watching an enormous amount of ministry getting done by others.

How It Works

What is behind the unusual dynamic of the 120 Fellowship? I have meditated on this for some time, and three areas keep surfacing in my mind by way of explanation. They are prayer, commitment, and ministry.

Prayer. I always have believed in prayer. I always have practiced it, although not on a level I have been particularly satisfied with. But because of the ministry of several members of the 120 Fellowship, I now have begun to understand the *power* of prayer for the first time in my life.

A while ago my pastor, Paul Cedar, asked, "What is the secret of the 120 Fellowship?"

"Prayer!" I immediately said.

My answer was much more than a pious platitude. Prayer can have dramatic effects, as I have seen in my own life. In the 120 Fellowship, we have several members with the special gift of intercession; some without the gift but who discipline themselves to pray for requests regularly; an emergency prayer chain; a meaningful time of prayer in each class session; and a team, led by George Eckart, which prays with unusual power for the sick and needy for at least one hour after every class period.

Commitment. I don't believe that anyone in our class feels we are as committed as we should be. But, while there always is room for improvement, I can honestly say the commitment level is at least above average. As a starter, the class meets at 7:30 on Sunday morning and runs until 9:15. Getting up at that time on Sunday does not come naturally to many people. We have breakfast together, we spend a lot of time in sharing, we pray for each other, and we have a Bible lesson which usually involves a good bit of class discussion. Most class members are there because they believe they can contribute something to others. That leads to the third dynamic.

Ministry. The 120 Fellowship believes in the theology of the Body of Christ. Each member has been given one or more spiritual gifts in order to contribute to the well-being of the whole body. In leading the class I give high priority to helping each person discover, develop, and use his or her spiritual gift. For example, the class president, David Anderson, has a gift of administration which is a tremendous benefit to me. My worries about how the class is being run are nil. I also have discovered that twelve class members have the gift of pastoring: eight women and four men. One of the women, Cathy Schaller, leads the team. They, as well as others who are discovering the same gift, make sure the pastoral needs of the whole flock are met. My stated objective is that the needs of the members of the 120 Fellowship will be so well met by the class itself that they will rarely, if ever, need to consult the professional pastoral staff of the church.

Does this threaten the professional pastoral staff? By no means. They also understand and promote the theology of the Body of Christ and affirm what is happening. I feel that the 120 Fellowship is a concrete example of how the ministry of the Holy Spirit in the Third Wave can become a part of traditional evangelical churches. It is an integral part of a traditional mainstream evangelical church, which has not particularly had a history of this type of activity.

I sense that what God is doing here, he also is doing in many other churches around the country. The decade of the '80s is proving to be the one when the miraculous power of the Holy Spirit is beginning to flow in churches which are non-Pentecostal and noncharismatic. This is a manifestation of what I am calling the Third Wave. So far I am aware of only a few other instances, but perhaps more news will come in.

Principles for Ministry

I also sense that God wants to multiply this type of ministry in our day. This is what motivates me to share how it is being done at our Lake Avenue church. I do not consider the 120 Fellowship a model for all others to imitate. But it may be an example for some in similar circumstances. Six very important principles have allowed it to happen.

The senior pastor. This is first in importance. I have tremendous respect, based on biblical teaching, for the leadership and authority of the senior pastor. I have argued the point as strongly as I can in my book *Leading Your Church to Growth.* If God has not opened the senior pastor to it, I do not recommend experimenting with a Third Wave ministry. It can split a church. While our pastor, Paul Cedar, is neither a Pentecostal nor a charismatic, he nevertheless is open to the movement of the Holy Spirit and very supportive of the 120 Fellowship.

Worship. It is important never to become a "church within a church." We stress the need for every member of the class to be a responsible member of the church as a whole. We also purposely do not hold a competitive worship service in our class. We rarely sing. We do most of our singing and worshiping with the whole congregation at the 9:30 service. On class retreats and in some of the small groups which meet in homes during the week we do hold extended times of worship and praise, but rarely on Sunday morning.

Giving. Our church believes in tithing plus. Our pastor teaches that we should give ten percent of our income to the church and that we should give generously over and above that for other causes which the Lord lays on our hearts. We have many class projects in the 120 Fellowship which require a large monthly cash flow. But we do not permit any of the money donated to the class to be subtracted from money already promised to the church as a whole.

For instance, we were recently challenged to participate in ministry in Northwest Pasadena, an urban black ghetto with the highest daytime crime rate in our state. John Perkins, founder of the Voice of Calvary in Mississippi, recently moved into Northwest Pasadena to begin a new ministry. God led him to become a member of the 120 Fellowship, and this has drawn all of us into outreach to that area.

As a starter, a young white couple from the class, Fritz and Nanette Brown, volunteered to give their summer to organizing a "Work Force" to provide employment for teenagers out of school. They estimated that they would need a budget of $4,500 to do it. The 120 Fellowship set aside a Work Force Sunday for a special offering. A surprising $6,000 was given or pledged that day. But that was all over and above what each of us regularly gives to the church.

Communication. We believe we need to be open and aboveboard in all that happens in the class. We especially try to keep wide-open channels of communication with our pastoral staff. We publish a monthly newsletter called *Body Life,* and make sure our pastors receive a copy. Our Pastor of Lay Ministries, Ray Syrstad, meets once a month with me and with the other adult Sunday School teachers. He also meets once a month with David Anderson, our class president, along with his counterparts from other classes. We make sure that we are an integral part of the overall Sunday School program of the church and not something separate from it. We do not want anything we do in our class to come as a surprise to our pastoral leaders.

Terminology. We do not allow the 120 Fellowship to be called "charismatic," nor do I accept the label personally. I have nothing but admiration and praise for the so-called charismatic movement and for charismatics. I just prefer not to be one. I have explained some of the theological differences in my approach to the use of this term. At this point the reason for our semantic preference is largely social. Like it or not, many mainline evangelicals have developed strongly negative attitudes toward the charismatic movement over the past twenty years. Much of this has been caused by excesses with which most charismatics would not want to identify. But the attitude unfortunately has spread to cover the entire movement. Many of these evangelicals, however, are not negative toward the movement of the Holy Spirit. This is one reason I believe he now is coming on a Third Wave, different from the two earlier waves of Pentecostals and charismatics which continue strongly.

Modesty. We are under no illusion that what God is doing in the 120 Fellowship he wants to do for all Christians. We are seeing signs and wonders on a regular basis, but we also know that God is blessing many other churches which see no signs and wonders at all. We do not even think that we are setting a pattern for other adult Sunday School classes in our own church. There are twenty-one other adult classes attended by over 2,000 adults who love them. God is present, and their needs are being met. If they weren't, the Sunday

School wouldn't be growing at some ten percent per year.

This important point has been missed by some who have experienced the miraculous power of the Holy Spirit in the past. They have regarded themselves as superspiritual and have, often unintentionally, imposed a "guilt trip" on others. They have acted as if Christians who had not had similar experiences or who were not "Spirit-filled" were a notch or two below them on the spirituality scale. We are determined not to allow this to happen in the 120 Fellowship.

These six principles are not to be regarded as a formula which, once applied, will automatically produce a Third Wave group. But let them be a starting point for prayer, discussion, and action.

FIVE

Victory over Evil Spirits

A MONG THE SUPERNATURAL REALITIES we encounter in the movement of the Holy Spirit that I call the Third Wave, one of the hardest for the Western mindset to accept is the work of demons. The Bible, however, testifies to the reality of evil spirits. One of the things Jesus had to do most frequently was cast them out. From my own experience, and from that of other missionaries, I can testify that Satan is still active in the world today, and that Jesus still has the power to defeat him.

Evangelical Christians have many questions about the work of evil spirits. I believe that God has shown me enough to be able to suggest answers for some of them. Two questions in particular have implications for our ministry in fulfilling Jesus' great commission. The first concerns the power of evil spirits over particular areas or groups. The second concerns the ability of demons to harm Christian believers.

Demonic Principalities

Could it be possible that Satan, frequently referred to in Scripture as "the god of this age," assigns certain of the demonic spirits under him to promote the kingdom of darkness in given nations, cities, regions, cultural groups, or other segments of the world's population?

If the answer to this question is yes, it becomes obvious that it has tremendous implications for evangelism. If these ruling spirits can be identified and if their power can be broken through spiritual warfare on a high level, the preaching of the gospel of salvation will presumably have freer access to the hearts of those who are lost. The Apostle Paul speaks of those who are perishing "whose minds the god of this age has blinded, who do not believe, lest the light of the gospel of the glory of Christ, who is the image of God, should shine on them" (2 Cor 4:4). Apparently, one of the major objectives of the devil and his forces of evil is to blind people's eyes so they will not receive the gospel. But if somehow that power can be broken, blind eyes might then see the gospel and allow Jesus Christ to take possession of their lives.

For those of us called to fulfill the great commission, it is a line of thought worth pursuing. I do not presume to have all the answers on either the theoretical or the practical level, but I am very much interested in learning more about possible territorial hierarchies of demons.

We are told that "we do not wrestle against flesh and blood, but against principalities, against powers, against the rulers of the darkness of this age, against spiritual hosts of wickedness in the heavenly places" (Eph 6:12). That's the bad news. The good news is that they have already been defeated. The Bible says of Jesus on the cross: "Having disarmed principalities and powers, he made a public spectacle of them, triumphing over them in it" (Col 2:15). The ultimate defeat is certainly assured. But meanwhile there are still battles to be fought and mopping-up exercises to be carried out. The enemy is still blinding the eyes of millions of people around the world to the gospel of Christ. In light of this, it seems to be that the more we can learn about this wrestling match we are in, the more people around the world might ultimately be evangelized.

We get a clue from an interesting story in Daniel 10. Daniel the prophet, who was a captive in Persia at the time, entered into a period of prayer and fasting in order to receive a word from God. Finally, on the twenty-first day of the fast an angel appeared to him. He told Daniel that God had heard and answered his prayer the first day by sending an angel to him. But in order to get to Daniel, the angel had to battle "the prince of the kingdom of Persia." The battle lasted twenty-one days and did not finish until the angel Michael came to help him. Then he got through (Dn 10:12-13).

But that was not all. On his return trip the angel expected to fight again with the prince of Persia and he also expected a battle with the "prince of Greece" (Dn 10:20).

These references are only a clue. Daniel gives us no more details. But there is a strong possibility that the princes in Daniel have something to do with the principalities and powers of Ephesians and Colossians. If so, we might at least work on the hypothesis that certain demonic personalities do control certain territories of the world.

I was interested to read an article called "Waging War" by Bill Jackson in an issue of *World Christian* magazine (1985, vol. 4, no. 1).

He tells of the experiences of a retired missionary couple from Thailand. Like many missionaries in that nation, they had labored long and faithfully, but with meager results. Then they entered into a new phase of ministry. They realized that the basic reason why the gospel was not penetrating might be that evil spirits were controlling the people. So they set aside one day a week for spiritual warfare. They went out to bind the demons and loose God's Spirit. What happened? "Before long, they saw God begin to heal and change lives in a tangible and powerful way. They eventually experienced a wave of conversions among that people."

It seems that this missionary couple learned power evangelism. Whether there are certain principles or even techniques for engaging in power evangelism related to demonic control of territories, I am not yet prepared to say. I have been in contact with some who feel there are, and I am learning from them.

An increasing number of field reports from people sensitive to these issues are coming in. For example, Ralph Mahoney of World MAP tells of a missionary whose travels took him to a small rural town situated on the Uruguay-Brazil border. In fact the national boundary ran along the main street. He began distributing tracts on the Uruguayan side of the street in the morning, but encountered resistance.

Discouraged, the missionary crossed over to the Brazilian side of the street and much to his surprise the people gratefully accepted the literature and some even stopped to read it right on the spot. Then he noticed that a woman who had refused a tract on the Uruguayan side crossed over to the Brazilian side and began window shopping. The missionary waited for her and as she approached offered her the tract once again. She smiled, took it and thanked him profusely. He tested several others and many followed the same pattern.

Later as he was praying about the incident, the words of Jesus came to his mind: "No one can enter a strong man's house and plunder his goods, unless he first binds the strong man, and then he will plunder the house" (Mk 3:27). Could it be that the "strong man" on the Brazilian side had been bound while the "strong man" on the Uruguayan side was still exercising power?

Another illustration of demonic control of territories comes from a report brought by my colleague, Charles Kraft, professor in the School of World Missions at Fuller Seminary, from a recent trip to Costa Rica. There he met a Christian psychiatrist, Rita Cabezas de Krumm, who uses a ministry of deliverance for many of her patients. Mrs. Krumm videotaped several sessions with a patient named Odilia, 54. As the sessions progressed, the demons in Odilia manifested themselves several times.

There are numerous details associated with this rather extended therapy which I won't mention. But in the fifth month of treatment Odilia made a trip to the United States. There she felt perfectly well, but as soon as she returned to Costa Rica the seizures began again. Apparently the demons had stayed in her house and had entered her again when she had returned.

Not that the United States has no demons. There seem to be territories assigned to them here too.

In April 1985, a major conference was held in Houston, Texas, called the National Convocation on Evangelizing Ethnic America. In one workshop I heard a fascinating story from Herman Williams, a Navajo Indian pastor working with the Christian and Missionary Alliance.

At the time Williams lived in a remote part of the Navajo reservation. He became seriously ill and decided to go to the hospital. On the way to the hospital with his wife their truck crossed the reservation boundary. Instantly he was perfectly healthy. It was embarrassing because they had called ahead of time and made an appointment with the doctor. Nevertheless, he cancelled the appointment, did some shopping, and drove toward home. The moment they entered the reservation the illness came back with all its intensity. He went to bed, but couldn't sleep.

In the night he heard an Indian singing in his house. His wife also heard it. The singing and the beating of a drum were coming from the kitchen wall. Three nights later the same thing happened. As he went into the kitchen he heard an inner voice, which he interpreted to be the Holy Spirit, tell him to rebuke what was in the wall. He did. The noise stopped and he was instantly healed from his sickness.

The next morning he was called to the home of the medicine man urgently. The man was twisted up in a corner of the house with the same illness Williams had contracted. By 10:00 he was dead. Pastor Williams later discovered that the medicine man had put a curse on him.

How all the details of an incident like this are to be interpreted I am not sure. But for one thing, there seemed to be a power of evil operating on one side of the reservation border and not on the other side. In a later interview, Herman Williams said to me, "There is a demon prince over each Indian village."

I keep struggling with what to do with these kinds of reports. We have the authority that Jesus has given us over evil. But just how to exercise this authority over the principalities and powers binding a certain territory and releasing that territory for the expansion of the gospel and the kingdom of God is, at least for me, still an unanswered question.

If there is an answer it will undoubtedly be a form of power evangelism. Elusive as it might be, I believe it is worth pursuing. Meanwhile our responsibility is to put on the full armor of God.

Can Demons Harm Christians?

Some Christian leaders involved in a deliverance ministry have asserted that true born-again Christians can be indwelt by real live demons. Some other Christians have protested against this teaching. I suppose they have in mind the Scripture, "Greater is he that is in you than he that is in the world" (1 Jn 4:4).

This is one area in which I have learned much by personal experiences which God has allowed. I now feel certain that the power of evil spirits is real and can have direct influence in the life of a Christian.

We live in Altadena, California, in a house over sixty years old. We have lived in it seventeen years, and have no idea what went on in the house before we moved in.

Members of my Sunday School class, the 120 Fellowship, come to our house occasionally for a night of intercession. On one of those nights two people who have the gift of discernment of spirits sensed something wrong in the house, especially in our bedroom. So they went upstairs and prayed against the evil they felt was there. Whether anything happened at the moment, I do not know.

Not long afterward, in the middle of one night when I was away, my wife Doris woke up with a terrible fear. Her heart was pounding. She opened her eyes to see a luminous green outline of some being in the corner of the room. She could see a pair of eyes, also luminous green. She recognized that it was an evil spirit and rebuked it in the name of Jesus. First she commanded it to leave the room. Then, not wanting it to go into one of the children's rooms, she commanded it to leave the house. It moved a few feet to the right, then back again, then disappeared. Doris went back to bed and slept soundly the rest of the night with complete peace.

A couple of months later, when I was home, Doris woke up in the night with a horrible, piercing cramp in her foot. She tried to work it out but couldn't so she woke me up and asked me to pray for it. I laid my hand on her foot and prayed against the pain and cramp. For ten minutes we tried to get back to sleep, but the pain would not leave.

"I think it's a spirit," Doris said. So I prayed again, this time rebuking the spirit in the name of Jesus. The pain went and did not come back.

The next episode occurred after two members of my Sunday School class who have a powerful ministry of healing and deliverance, George Eckart and Cathy Schaller, were talking to Doris. She mentioned the green spirit. They immediately suggested that they go to our house to check it out. Because my wife and I were both at work, they got the house key from her and went to our home.

George and Cathy got out of the car and opened the gate to a small courtyard in front of the house, but they could not go any farther. Some powerful physical force was resisting them. So instead of going to the front door, they entered the garage. There was such a tremendous energy that Cathy could actually smell the evil. (She had smelled something similar before, so this was not a new experience.) They found the spirit and cast it out.

In the process, Cathy looked on a wall where I had some garden tools hanging. When she saw the ax, she had a strong sense of violence. This became significant later on.

When they finished in the garage, the force that had kept them out of the courtyard no longer was there, so they entered the house.

Here again they sensed the presence of evil. As he had prayed before coming to the house, George had a vision of some kind of stone idol shaped like an animal. He didn't understand the significance of this until in the living room he saw the real thing on a table. It was a stone puma which we had brought home from Bolivia where we served as missionaries. The spirit in the living room moved around, but George and Cathy were aware of it and pursued it until it left. Needless to say, when Doris and I got home that evening we took that puma as well as two pagan ceremonial masks we also foolishly had brought with us and smashed them to bits.

This was new to us, so we asked George and Cathy how they knew for sure there was a certain spirit in a certain room. They told us that in each instance, completely independent from each other, God showed them both where the spirits were at exactly the same time. There was no doubt whatsoever in their minds.

They found nothing else downstairs, so they went upstairs. They rated our daughter Becky's room relatively free of evil, but prayed against any waging oppression. Then they went to our bedroom. There they sensed a demonic presence as strong as that in the garage.

But another strange thing happened there. George saw a vision in the exact spot where my wife had seen the spirit. It was a vivid scene of a man with an ax involved in great violence. In his spirit he heard a loud scream which appeared to come from a woman. Cathy confirmed that it was a reflection of the impression she had received when she had seen the ax in the garage. Whether a murder had been committed there or not, George could not be sure.

All this occurred a few years ago. So far as we know, the house is clean. I'm not sure where all the demons came from, but I do suspect that we brought some of them back from Bolivia. Like many missionaries, we were so naive we did not realize that demons could and would attach themselves to objects and also to persons. We since have run into American Christians who have picked up spirits by visiting pagan temples as tourists in other countries. This might well have happened to me, because on my trips abroad I used to visit some of these places. Wherever it was, I did pick up a wicked spirit that caused me severe pain for ten years until I discovered what it was and dealt with it.

In 1973 I began getting migraine headaches. They increased in intensity until I had a whopper which lasted seventy days and seventy nights without stopping.

I did everything I knew to get relief. I underwent extensive treatment by one of Southern California's most famous chiropractors. I changed my diet. I revised my exercise routine. I learned about acupressure points. I began getting more rest by sleeping later in the mornings (until then my awakening time had been 4:30 A.M.). I read books on headaches and their treatment. I took vitamins. I tried all kinds of pain killers in all kinds of doses. Nothing really helped.

Finally I discovered a Canadian drug called "222"

which, if I exceeded the recommended dosage, would give me some relief. So whenever my students would come to Fuller Seminary from Canada, I would ask them to bring me two or three bottles of "222."

By 1980 it was not unusual for me to have a headache five out of seven days every week. Fortunately the headaches were not completely debilitating like some migraines. If I took enough "222" and applied enough courage and persistence I usually could move through my daily routine and many people would not even know I was in pain.

When I began experiencing the power of the Holy Spirit about three or four years ago, I would ask people with the gift of healing to pray for me. Sometimes—but not always—I would get a few days of temporary relief. One of those who prayed was my friend Paul Yonggi Cho, pastor of the world's largest church in Seoul, Korea, who laid hands on me after I preached in his church one Sunday. But I still had the headaches five days out of seven.

Then in November 1982 I attended Vineyard Christian Fellowship of Anaheim on a Sunday night as I occasionally do. The pastor is my colleague, John Wimber. After John preached, several people spoke words of knowledge, one indicating that someone there was suffering with migraine headaches caused by a tumor in the brain which had not been diagnosed as such. It so happened that it was one of those days I did not have a headache, but I responded anyway, hoping God would minister to me.

A group gathered around me and began to pray. As

they prayed, I felt the hand of one of them suddenly push my head.

"There it goes," he said.

Since I had no headache, I didn't know for sure if anything had happened or not. But after the meeting John Wimber came up to me.

"My friend says your problem is a spirit," he said.

I let it go at that, went home, and still had headaches five days out of seven.

Then our MC510 class met in January 1983. Sure enough, the first Monday night I went to class with a headache. So during the break I asked John to pray for me. John and his wife, Carol, prayed for me. The pain left. But about an hour later it was back again.

"How is your headache?" John asked after class.

"It went away but came back," I replied.

"Don't forget about that spirit," he said.

"O.K.," I said. "But what am I supposed to do about it?"

John replied quickly, "Treat it like a cat on the back porch! Yell at it and tell it to go away!"

That gave me a problem. As a Christian I was used to talking to God whom I cannot see. But I was not used to talking to anyone else I couldn't see. Furthermore, I thought, God is omniscient and can hear our silent prayers, but demons do not have that attribute. They cannot read our minds. We must speak to them out loud

Because I didn't want people to think I was crazy, J kept quiet.

A few days later I was in the shower early in the

morning and the symptoms of a headache began. It always started in exactly the same place on the back of my head.

I said, "Oh, no . . . another headache," and planned to take "222" when I got out of the shower. Then it dawned on me that I was all alone. My wife was still in bed. The shower was making plenty of noise, and no one would think I was crazy. So I went for it and treated the spirit like a cat on the back porch. I rebuked it in the name of Jesus and told it to get out of there once and for all.

Being an absentminded professor, I forgot about the whole thing until about 10:30 that morning. Suddenly I realized that I did not have a headache!

That was the beginning of the end. For some years after that I did not take even an aspirin for any kind of headache at all.

I say the beginning, because many times, with great frequency at first, the spirit tried to come back and harass me. The beginning headache symptoms would come, but on each occasion I told it that it could not come back and commanded it to leave.

As a footnote, the headaches came back somewhat when I suffered with the flu a couple of years ago, but, through prayer, they left. Friends with the gift of discernment did not believe the second round was associated with evil spirits.

It is true that the Holy Spirit, who is within us, is greater than the devil, who is in the world. But I am learning that the power of the Holy Spirit is not always activated automatically. The devil has power to attack us, and that is why we are susceptible to his attacks even if we may be Christians, ordained ministers, missionaries, or seminary professors.

Part of the excitement I am feeling in the Third Wave is learning little by little how this spiritual battle is being fought and what it means to put on the full armor of God. I am far from knowing what I need to know, but I am trusting fully in God who is directing the process in his own way and in his own time.

Awareness of Demons

While Satan has been defeated, he is not totally destroyed, nor will he be until the fulfillment of Revelation 20:10 when he and his friends are cast into the lake of fire. I think he can be likened to a hunted lion which has received a load of buckshot in the intestines. He may be mortally wounded, but the time between being shot and dying is the time the beast is most dangerous.

In my research, I have noticed several things. For one, almost all those who themselves are actively involved in a ministry of exorcism or deliverance affirm that Christians can be demonized. Those who deny it, by and large, have had little or no direct contact with the demonic.

For another, I have discovered that several Christian leaders have changed their opinion on this matter over the years. But the changes I have found have all been in the same direction: from once denying that demons can harm Christians to now affirming that they can and do. As of yet, I have not known of those who have changed from believing that demons harm Christians to not believing it anymore.

For example, Charles Swindoll, author of a number of Christian best sellers and pastor of First Evangelical Free Church of Fullerton, California, has changed his opinion. In a booklet entitled *Demonism*, he raises the question, "Can a Christian be demonized?" His answer: "For a number of years, I questioned this, but I am now convinced it can occur. . . . Wicked forces are not discriminating with regard to which body they may inhabit." Swindoll asserts that through the years he has worked with troubled, anguished Christians. And "on a few occasions I have assisted in the painful process of relieving them of demons."

Southern Baptist evangelist James Robison says there was a time when he did not believe that Christians needed deliverance from demonic oppression. Looking back, he now says, "I never dreamed that I needed to be delivered, but for years I was tormented by the devil." He confesses that, while engaged in a successful evangelistic ministry, he was tormented by covetousness, lust, anger, gluttony, unforgiveness and many other sins to an extraordinary degree. Then, through the ministry of a discerning friend, Milton Green, he was delivered from what he perceived to be a demonic claw, and from that moment he was a free man.

One of my good friends through the years has been Edward Murphy, missionary to Latin America, former professor at Biola University and now vice-president of Overseas Crusades. Murphy says, "It used to be thought—and I made this assumption just like everyone else—that the moment the Holy Spirit entered a new Christian's life, the evil spirits, if there were any there, were automatically expelled." His missionary experience, however, forced him to change his mind.

"I have found," says Murphy, "that people can come to Christ in a genuine salvation experience and still have problems in the demonic realm." Murphy now has a regular ministry of delivering individuals, Christians included, from evil spirits.

We can take authority over the demonic in Jesus' name. We have the Holy Spirit in us who is more than sufficient to ward off the roaring lion, whether it has been hit by buckshot or not. Most Christians I know are not demonized because their shield of faith quenches the fiery darts of the wicked one. But where Satan has broken through to harass, I want to be among those who recognize it and, through the power of the Holy Spirit, put a stop to it.

The Bible does not say, "Ignore Satan and he will flee from you." It tells us that he flees when we *resist* him. Recognizing who he is and what he does is the first step in intelligent resistance.

SIX

Your Worldview
Makes a Difference

I ONCE SAT IN ON A FASCINATING EXAMINATION. The
faculty of a respected American seminary was questioning a prospective faculty member on his theological
views. The candidate was Chinese.

The first question was, "What is your general impression of our statement of faith?"

"I think it is a fine, evangelical statement as far as it
goes," he replied. "It may be adequate for a Western
seminary, but not for an Asian institution."

His response provoked a long series of follow-up
questions. The upshot was that the statement of faith
had no section on supernatural forces of good and evil
such as angels and demons. It had mentioned Satan in
passing, but contained no explicit reference to his
personality or work in the world today. To the Asian
believer, it failed to reflect an important area of biblical
revelation.

Very few statements of faith belonging to American
churches, denominations, and parachurch organiza-

tions bring up the dimensions of the working of the supernatural in daily experience. They frequently mention the work of the Holy Spirit in saving souls, but not in healing bodies. They mention the Spirit's power for living a godly life, but not for casting out demons.

Why is this?

In my opinion, it stems mainly from our traditional Anglo-American worldview which is increasingly materialistic and naturalistic. Secular materialism has penetrated our Christian institutions to a surprising degree. This is not to say we have an *atheistic* worldview. No. A large majority of Americans believe there is a God, and many know him personally through Jesus Christ. But our worldview is heavily influenced by secular science. We are taught to believe that almost everything which happens in daily life has causes and effects which are governed by scientific laws.

God and the supernatural are much more distant to us than to the average person from the Third World, for instance. Most people out there, representing over two-thirds of humanity, have no doubt that much of their daily experience is determined by the whims of demons and evil spirits which are not bound by the laws of nature. Their worldview tells them shamans, witches, witch doctors, and mediums have the power to control the supernatural forces which cause disease, poverty, oppression, crop failure, hurricanes, barrenness, drought, and mental illness. When Christianity comes along, the uppermost question in their minds is whether its God has enough power to solve life's problems.

Despite the inability of many Western missionaries to

relate to such questions and concerns, the gospel is spreading rapidly in many parts of the world. Large numbers of people are becoming followers of Jesus Christ in Asia, Africa, and Latin America. This is the good news.

There is some bad news as well. An unexpected problem is surfacing. A short while ago the Inter-denominational Foreign Mission Association (IFMA) and the Evangelical Foreign Missions Association (EFMA) held a joint study conference at the U.S. Center for World Mission in Pasadena, California. Ron Blue, professor of missions at Dallas Theological Seminary, gave one of the plenary addresses. In it he reported that one of the chief problems among the believers in the churches planted by evangelical missions in Africa was a frighteningly large number of Christian believers who still rely on the witch doctor whenever a serious problem comes into their lives.

This surprised me, so I glanced over at Charles Kraft and Dean Gilliland, our two African specialists from the Fuller School of World Mission. Both were nodding their heads in agreement. They later told me that at Fuller one of our African students from Zaire is doing a whole doctoral dissertation on this critical issue.

How could this happen? We are not talking about new converts, babes in Christ, who go to the witch doctor. We are talking about mature believers, elders, Sunday School teachers, and even pastors.

The explanation is fairly simple. Our Western seminaries and Bible colleges sent out missionaries who were not trained to deal with these problems of what is known as the "middle zone" because of the worldview reflected in the doctrinal statements which I referred to earlier. This was precisely the concern of the Chinese professor who came with a different worldview.

A growing number of Christians around the world are beginning to recognize that the gospel which was taken to them was the authentic gospel, but it was not the whole gospel. When many missionaries set up pastoral training institutions in the Third World, they based their curricula on the Western worldview also.

By pointing this out, I am not attacking the missionaries. How could I? Let the one who is without sin throw the first stone. All of my American missionary colleagues on the Fuller School of World Mission faculty have been field missionaries. And all of us, to one degree or another, have made the errors I am describing.

Professor Dean Gilliland, for instance, tells us how a Nigerian pastor once came to him for help with his wife who was demonized.

"I felt like I was teaching the Bible with one hand tied behind my back," Gilliland says. "I couldn't help him, so the pastor had to resort to the pagan witch doctor who covered his wife with a blanket, waved a banana stalk over her, and gave her what help he could."

New Testament Worldview

My heart is for world evangelization. This is why I am so concerned that the message we preach in the world is one which makes sense to the worldview of the people to whom we preach. Checking back into the New

Testament, I find the worldview of the people in those days, both Jews and Greeks, was much more akin to the worldview of the Third World than to our Western secularized way of understanding reality.

This worldview played a major role in one of the most astounding historical phenomena ever recorded: the spread of Christianity in the early centuries. It began with 120 in the upper room around 33 A.D. Within three centuries it had become the predominant religion of the Roman Empire.

What brought this about?

The answer to that question is clearer than it ever has been thanks to Yale University historian Ramsay MacMullen, author of *Christianizing the Roman Empire, A.D. 100-400* (Yale University Press). A great value of this book is MacMullen's perspective. He is not writing as a Christian theologian arguing a point, but simply as an objective secular historian telling it like it is.

Early in his book, MacMullen raises what he considers a most important question: "What *did* Christianity present to its audience? For plainly the process of conversion that interests me took place in people's minds on the basis of what they knew, or thought they knew." The answer is deceptively simple. While Christianity was being presented to unbelievers in both word and deed, it was the deed that far exceeded the word in evangelistic effectiveness.

The people of the Roman Empire were not secular humanists. They knew about miracles and took them for granted. "*Not* to believe in them would have made you seem more than odd, simply irrational, as it would have seemed irrational seriously to suppose that babies are brought by storks," MacMullen says. They expected the gods they believed in to perform miracles, and they did. They healed people, pronounced oracles, made it rain, helped them win wars, and cursed their enemies.

Early Christian missionaries and preachers would not have questioned the miraculous power of pagan gods in the slightest. Their point was that this is the power of the kingdom of darkness, directly caused by demons which the Romans gullibly had been calling "gods." Furthermore, the end result of that power was to bring evil and suffering in the present life, and worst of all, eternal death.

The Christian God, Father of Jesus Christ, was presented first and foremost as a God who works miracles. His power was declared to be greater than the power of the pagan gods. It was a power for good, not evil, and it promised eternal life. MacMullen points out that in the early centuries very few pagans were converted because of Christian doctrine or because of logical presentations of truth. Christianity swept through the Roman Empire because the people could see with their own eyes that Jesus did miracles greater than any gods they had known of.

Christian preachers in those days were so sure of the power of God that they did not hesitate to engage in power encounters. They would challenge in public the power of pagan gods with the power of Jesus. MacMullen relates many of these. For instance, he tells how the author of the apocryphal Acts of Peter provoked a spiritual "shootout" in the very forum of the capital. It was done "after a great deal of braggadocio and confrontational theatrics in previous days, and statements for the press, and in the presence of a highly interested crowd."

All this involved "the manhandling of demons—humiliating them, making them howl, beg for mercy, tell their secrets, and depart in a hurry." By the time the Christian preachers got through, no one would want to worship such "nasty, lower powers."

MacMullen tells a story of John the Apostle that is not well-known to Christians because it is not in the Bible. It is told in the apocryphal Acts of John and takes place in Ephesus. Great acts of healing won many of the people in Ephesus. But the power encounter came in the temple of the goddess Artemis, apparently the seat of the chief prince of the demons who had jurisdiction over Ephesus.

In the temple, according to the author of the Acts of John, John prayed, "O God ... at whose name every idol takes flight and every demon and every unclean power, now let the demon that is here take flight in Thy name." As soon as he said that, the altar of Artemis split in pieces, and half of the whole temple fell down.

"We are converted now that we have seen thy marvelous works," the Ephesians said.

When I was in seminary I was taught not to put much stock in these apostolic-times stories which weren't in the Bible. MacMullen disagrees with that. As a historian, he believes such stories are reliably reported and can be taken as historically important. Furthermore, he finds, they were widely used to bring people to conversion to Christianity.

When dramatic events happened like the power encounter in Ephesus, "listeners were and should have been scared half to death," MacMullen affirms. "Divine power had a terrifying, high-voltage quality that split and blinded." He concludes that the supernatural power of God "driving all competition from the field" should be seen as "the chief instrument of conversion" in those first centuries.

For one thing, this remarkable book helps dispel possible doubts that the supernatural power of God continued after the days of the apostles. Historical research is showing that there never was a time when miracles ceased, particularly on the frontiers where the gospel of the kingdom was penetrating new groups. In the past, few historians discussed it. MacMullen cites another historian of the period, Peter Brown, who points out how historians have minimized the record of the miraculous in early Christianity. "In so doing," says Brown, "they have declared the study of exorcism, possibly the most highly rated activity of the early Christian church, a historiographical 'no-go' area." No longer—especially since Ramsay MacMullen has pioneered the field. His research will go a long way to open up the horizons of many today who all too long have been captives of a worldview oriented to secular humanism and, thereby, shut off from a huge segment of reality which, when allowed to operate, can bring life, hope, and peace.

Seeing Jesus

When the message of Jesus in its original context meets the supernatural worldview of the Third World, some amazing things can happen. People simply take Jesus at his word, and signs and wonders follow. One example of this effect is the film *Jesus,* produced by Campus Crusade for Christ, which clearly is turning out to be one of the most powerful evangelistic tools of the decade.

Jesus is a two hour professional production. With the financial backing of Bunker Hunt and the expertise of John Heyman and Warner Brothers (film producers), *Jesus* has turned out to be in a class of its own as far as an authentic portrayal of the life of the Savior is concerned. One of the major contributors to the authenticity is the dialogue. Every word spoken by Jesus in the film is taken directly from the Gospel of Luke.

The original film was produced in English. It was the fulfillment of a vision which God had given Bill Bright, president of Campus Crusade, in the 1940s. Bright knew that with less than half the earth's population functionally literate, the written word would not be adequate to complete the task of world evangelization. He felt that the spoken word, illustrated by a high-quality motion picture, would be the most likely medium for reaching millions who otherwise might not hear.

Bright prayed about the film for thirty years. Then in 1976, the year of Here's Life America, answers began to come. God signaled that his divine timing had arrived.

The exciting story of how the film was produced, and of the ministry it currently is having worldwide, is told in *I Just Saw Jesus* (Here's Life Publishers), one of the most remarkable evangelistic books of recent times. Its author is Paul Eshleman, Campus Crusade executive in charge of the project.

One of the most fascinating aspects of *I Just Saw Jesus* is Eshleman's analysis of repeated spontaneous releases of supernatural power for signs and wonders as a result of the film. The film is so realistic that many people, particularly in the Third World, feel they are seeing Jesus in person. And the Jesus they see, of course, regularly performs miracles: healing, deliverance from demons, feeding multitudes, raising the dead, and stilling the storm. The impression they receive is that manifestations of miraculous power are part of everyday Christianity.

Eshleman admits that to most of us Western believers, this kind of ministry is "a little hard to believe." But, he says, "Not so among the new believers! To those who know nothing more of Jesus than what they see in the film, it seems perfectly logical that the miracles they witness in *Jesus* might have occurred last week. If Jesus could do those things for the people of the village He visited in the picture, is there any reason to believe He cannot do the same for them?"

And what happens when people out there see *Jesus*?

They expect Jesus to do miracles today. And he does. Eshleman tells story after story of New Testament types of healings and deliverances which result in great harvests of souls.

In the Solomon Islands, doctors had given up on a little girl who was dying. The *Jesus* film came to town and the parents took their daughter for entertainment—to get their minds on something else. They saw Jesus raise Jairus' daughter from the dead. So that night when they put their daughter to bed they prayed he would do it again. The next morning she was perfectly well, and the doctors were baffled.

In Thailand, a group of believers was miraculously delivered from bandits known to murder their victims, and robbers were halted in their tracks by the physical appearance of two angels with flaming swords. In another part of Thailand, the film team slept in a Buddhist temple known locally to be inhabited by demons. They were awakened by a demon which appeared in a corner of the room as "the most frightful image they had ever seen." They cast it out in the name of Jesus, as they had seen in the film, and slept undisturbed the rest of the night, much to the aston-ishment of the villagers.

In India, evil spirits sent by the Sathya Sai Baba kept blowing the projector bulbs until they were forced to stop by the power of God.

A dramatic power encounter, reminiscent of Elijah's on Mount Carmel, involved a witch doctor in Mandala, India. He took home a flyer with a picture of Jesus and put it on a shelf with pictures of many other gods. He was beginning to believe that Jesus was the true God, but he needed a test. So he placed a tiny ball of dried cow dung fuel in front of each picture, believing that the most powerful one would ignite the fuel. Almost immediately the dung in front of Jesus' picture burst into flames. He is now a fervent evangelist for Jesus Christ.

In many places the ministry of the *Jesus* film results not only in conversions—each day an estimated 15,000 persons worldwide indicate their desire to receive Christ—but also in multiplying new churches. In the past few years in Thailand alone, some 700 churches are reported to have been formed by Campus Crusade personnel. This is all the more remarkable because Thailand has traditionally been a resistant nation.

Eshleman also tells of a growing church of more than 200 Muslim converts in Pamongan, Indonesia.

In Whitefield, India, Nazarene pastor S. Dinakaran showed the film in 30 villages over a 40 day period, to the entire population of 33,000. Approximately 23,000 now have seen it twice. From that have come four churches and five prayer cells on their way to becoming churches, with powerful miracles continuing on an almost daily basis.

Our worldview really does make a difference. If we recognize the whole of reality, like the early Christians or like these new Christians in the Third World, we can see Jesus in a whole new way. We can also see his power at work as it did in biblical times.

SEVEN

Power Evangelism

THE PHRASE "POWER EVENGELISM," first popularized by John Wimber, is receiving increasing attention from Christian leaders here in the United States and around the world. But the meaning of the term is in constant danger of being twisted out of proportion. Supernatural power often turns out to be so dramatic that the "power" draws all the attention, leaving the "evangelism" side of the formula to be virtually ignored.

That is why we must continually remind ourselves that the power of God to heal the sick, cast out demons, and perform miracles is not given as an end in itself.

God's power should be seen as a means to an end. The end is that God is glorified through reconciling people to himself.

Having said this, I am proud to be among those who are advocating power evangelism as an important tool for fulfilling the great commission in our day. One of the reasons I am so enthusiastic is that it is working. Across the board, the most effective evangelism in today's world is accompanied by manifestations of supernatural power.

By "effective evangelism," I am not necessarily referring to huge crusades or large numbers of "decisions for Christ." No, I refer to fruit that remains. Those who come to Christ through *effective* evangelism are those who become responsible members of local churches. True commitment to Christ involves simultaneous commitment to the body of Christ. That is why, in my opinion, effective evangelism should be measured by church growth.

For several months I have been involved in researching the worldwide church growth related to the Pentecostal and charismatic movements. I am discovering that three kinds of things are happening simultaneously:

1. There is some dramatic church growth without signs and wonders. I think, for example, of the multiplication of congregations belonging to the Evangelical Churches of West Africa in Nigeria. Not that signs and wonders have been totally absent, but they have not been encouraged through the ministry or teaching of the missionaries of the Sudan Interior Mission which gave birth to this denomination.

2. There are notable public displays of signs and wonders with little or no church growth following them. Some evangelists in Africa, for example, are seeing crowds of up to 150,000 per night for a week or more. The blind see, the dead are raised, the lame walk and demons are cast out. Many professions of faith are recorded. But six months after the crusade only a small fraction of those who accepted Christ are in the churches.

3. There is church growth with signs and wonders. This is real power evangelism as I understand it, and this is where most of the action currently is found. Here are some facts and figures on the status of power evangelism in the world today:

In its first fifty years the Pentecostal movement had grown to around 10 million worldwide. But in the next thirty-five years (1950-1985) it began to explode, soaring to over 240 million Pentecostals and charismatics today.

The nation with the most Pentecostals or charismatics is China, with 42.5 million. These, of course, are not denominationally identified as such, but power evangelism is a central characteristic of the life and outreach of these churches.

The Assemblies of God is the largest classical Pentecostal denomination in the world. In the ten years 1975 to 1985, the number of worldwide members and adherents has grown from 4,594,780 to 13,175,751, an increase of 296 percent.

Most of the vigorous growth of the Assemblies of God has come only in the last twenty years. However, it has been so dramatic that at the present time the Assemblies of God is the largest or second largest Protestant denomination in no fewer than thirty different countries of the world.

Currently there are over nine million Pentecostals or charismatics in the United States. At the current rates of growth the number could rise to fifteen million by 1990, and forty-one million by 2000.

The charismatic renewal movement in the mainline

churches, including both Protestant and Catholic, now numbers approximately 4.2 million in the United States.

Independent charismatic churches are currently the fastest growing segment of American religion.

Nine out of ten of the world's megachurches (several thousands) are Pentecostal or charismatic.

Pentecostal leaders occasionally quote their early adversaries who said, "This will soon blow over." "They were right" is the reply. "It has now blown over the whole world!" Truly, where people are tapping into God's resources for power evangelism, that is where today's action is.

No Exclusive Claims

Power evangelism, miracles, signs and wonders— these are not the exclusive property of Pentecostals or charismatics. God's power can't be contained by one group or denomination. In fact, power evangelism is spilling over, erasing the lines that have been there for so long.

You know what lines I mean. Most of us wish the lines were not there, but they are. Lines which define differences between Christians. Some are identified as evangelicals, some ecumenics, some charismatics, some Pentecostals, some liberals, some fundamentalists. The roots of power evangelism in the twentieth century are firmly set in the Pentecostal and charismatic movements. Evangelicals, who, generally speaking, share the passion for winning unbelievers to Christ with

Pentecostals and charismatics, have slowly begun to recognize that there may be both biblical and practical validity in evangelism accompanied with supernatural signs and wonders. But interest in either evangelism or power has been consistently low among those who find themselves on the left, or liberal, side of the theological spectrum.

This is what makes it noteworthy when an official journal of the World Council of Churches, head-quartered in Geneva, Switzerland, dedicates an entire issue to what we now call power evangelism. I refer to the April 1986 issue of *International Review of Mission,* a publication which ordinarily features articles relating to human brotherhood, Christian ecumenism, peace and justice, social ethics and left-wing political positions. But this one, as editor Eugene Stockwell puts it, proposes "to understand the charismatic experience more fully, and to see how all of us, whether or not we define ourselves as 'charismatics,' can learn about the empowering, enabling work of the Spirit in Christian mission today." I applaud this desire and feel that God will use it in a significant way in the days to come.

Anglican Bishop David Pytches, for example, tells of an incident in Chile, where he served as a missionary. A mentally ill woman in the town of Petraco was a public social menace. She would dash around wildly with a hatchet, threatening the townspeople. Her family, weary of keeping her tied down and restrained, con-sulted the small group of evangelical believers in the community. They called over a pastor from a neigh-boring town who came to Petraco and offered a public prayer for the woman. He said simply, "I cast this spirit from you in the name of Jesus." The woman fell as if dead, but soon got up and, in sound mind, praised the Lord.

That was the power. And the evangelism? People from all around the area heard of what had happened and poured into Petraco. Soon there were five new churches in the area. Pytches says, "That is a biblical pattern. . . . The church of God will grow wherever there are manifestations of God's power."

Roman Catholic priest Tom Forrest agrees. In the same issue of *International Review of Mission* he says if we are going to evangelize effectively, we must "seek and expect signs and wonders." Forrest believes that "if signs and wonders were necessary in Jesus' own task of evangelization, how much more so for us!"

Anglican Michael Harper affirms, *"Miracles help people believe."*

Most of the current emphasis on power evangelism is regarded as something brand new. To a significant extent, it is. However, when we read the New Testament, it occurs to us that it probably shouldn't be new. It was there all the time. But huge segments of Christianity, such as evangelicals and ecumenicals, have not been tuned into it. Why is this? Bishop Pytches tackles this question head on and suggests five reasons why many of us have lost sight of the need for signs and wonders in our evangelistic strategy planning.

1. *Our Western worldview, which is largely materialistic, blurs our perception of the spiritual world.* We need to tune in more to the worldview of Jesus and be open to the reality of the supernatural and miraculous.

2. *Ministering with signs and wonders sounds presumptuous to many.* Are we apostles? they ask. No, we are simply believers, but Jesus commissioned disciples just like us to minister as he did, with great power.

3. *We are frightened to see physical manifestations of the power of the Holy Spirit on individuals.* But most of this fear comes from lack of experience and it disappears when we become accustomed to ministering in supernatural power.

4. *We have a sense of powerlessness and don't want to look like fools.* It is true that we have little power, but Jesus said that when the Holy Spirit comes upon us we shall receive power. We need not hesitate to apply Jesus' power.

5. *We have no training, and, therefore, do not know how to minister in power.* This is true of most Christian leaders today, but steps are being taken to correct this deficiency in many of our seminaries and Bible schools.

Power evangelism is not the exclusive property of any one Christian group. It is something which God wants to do through the church as a whole whether left or right, in order to touch a lost world with the love of Jesus Christ.

Examples of Power Evangelism

Worldwide, however, there has been a growing trend since around 1950 toward power evangelism, especially in Asia, Africa, and Latin America. One of my personal goals is to research this and share, on as broad a scale as possible, what God is doing.

Recently, I had the privilege of visiting Argentina

where some of the world's most dramatic church growth now is taking place. This is unusual because Argentina traditionally has been one of the slowest of Latin American countries to receive the gospel. In the past few years, however, a substantial change has come, and Argentines now are some of the most responsive people. They are responding, more than to anything else, to power evangelism.

Two great movements of God are prominent in Argentina. One is a series of great evangelistic crusades called "Message of Salvation" under Carlos Annacondia. The other is the development of a fascinating, non-traditional church called "Vision of the Future" under Omar Cabrera.

Carlos Annacondia

Carlos Annacondia, is a Christian layperson, the owner of a nuts and bolts factory. In 1982 God began to speak to him about an evangelistic ministry, calling him to start preaching in the slums and then to hold crusades in suburbs of Buenos Aires. Wherever he has gone, he has left overflowing churches and thousands of people who have been healed, delivered from demonic oppression, and saved. Just before I arrived in Argentina, for example, he had held a crusade in the City of San Justo. The crusade had lasted for 40 nights, and 62,000 decisions for Christ were registered. Two weeks later one of the pastors reported that his attendance had multiplied five times and that his church building no longer was adequate. Many others had similar experiences.

God has given Annacondia an unusually powerful gift of exorcism or deliverance. He uses it both publicly and privately. One of the features of his crusades is a large yellow-striped tent about 150 feet long, used exclusively for casting out demons. He calls it the "spiritual intensive care unit." It is located about fifty feet behind the huge crusade platform set up in a vacant lot. The crusade site I visited was in the City of San Martin where they had secured a vacant lot of about ten acres. The platform is about forty feet long and six feet high, very well lighted, and equipped with a professional sound system.

A large area in front of the platform is roped off. It has tables to record decisions when the invitation is given. Around it are 2,000 chairs for the elderly and sick. Most of the people, up to nearly 100,000 per night, stand shoulder to shoulder during the whole meeting from 8:00 P.M. to midnight—four hours. There is so much spiritual power in the meetings, that when Annacondia gives the invitation, people literally run and push each other to get under the rope to the tables in order to register their decision for Christ.

One of the reasons for such freedom in people accepting Christ is that much of the satanic power over the immediate area previously has been broken. This is done toward the beginning of the meeting. After singing some praise choruses and giving an exhortation to the crowd, Annacondia prays a powerful prayer of deliverance over the whole audience. He addresses Satan in person and, in Jesus' name, breaks the power of the enemy. He prays long and hard until the demons present start manifesting themselves. Many people, sometimes hundreds, will fall to the ground, some under the power of evil, some under the power of the Holy Spirit.

A team of men has been trained to go throughout the audience urging those who are demonized to go to the tent. Many by this time cannot control themselves and have to be carried. Once the demonized arrive in the tent, another team of those gifted with a deliverance ministry takes over and begins to get rid of the demons. The tent sometimes becomes very noisy, as could be expected. Some of the difficult cases are ministered to until 3:00 or 4:00 or 5:00 in the morning. The team is all lay volunteers from the cooperating churches.

In addition to the teams trained to deal with the demonized, other large groups of lay volunteers are in charge of ushering, counseling, security, parking, traffic control, literature, maintenance, etc. Typically a crusade will use over 1,000 volunteers. Annacondia's own "Message of Salvation" staff consists of only eight full-time employees.

Annacondia reports that two particular manifestations of the Holy Spirit seem to impress unbelievers more than anything else in his crusades: falling in the power of the Spirit and filling teeth. On a fairly regular basis, decayed teeth are filled and new teeth grow where there were none before Interestingly, according to Annacondia, mostly unbelievers' teeth are filled; very few believers.

Spiritual power is so great that sometimes people simply passing by on the street will fall down. Most of those who do eventually receive Christ. Healings of all kinds occur nightly.

Omar Cabrera

Carlos Annacondia's work follows the pattern of classic crusade evangelism, with some important variations. Omar Cabrera, also uses crusades, or large public rallies, but in a non-traditional way.

Cabrera's rallies are part of the huge church he pastors, Vision of the Future. He travels from his headquarters in the City of Santa Fe and preaches twenty-five nights a month, mostly in public sports arenas. His dynamic wife, Marfa, sometimes accompanies him and directs parts of her husband's meetings. But ten or fifteen times a month, she herself preaches in other places. The church is unusual because it meets in forty different locations through the heavily populated central band of Argentina.

Cabrera is an eloquent, fiery public evangelist. His preaching spellbinds audiences which regularly run from 3,000 to 10,000 and more. Vision of the Future has 145,000 regular attenders, making it, on a world scale, one of the three largest churches.

Cabrera's preaching style is much like that of traditional crusade evangelists, but his mode of operation is significantly different on two major counts. While most crusade evangelists feel "called" to bring people to a decision for Jesus Christ, after the crusades they appear to have little personal pastoral concern for the converts. They prefer to leave the Christian-nurture ministry to others. They move from place to place, rarely returning to a city where they have held a crusade. Cabrera is different. He has established forty permanent locations and sees that sixty Vision of the Future meetings are held every month on a regular basis. Since Omar and Marfa Cabrera cannot preach at every meeting, they have recruited and trained a complex and efficient pastoral team to aid them. To start with, there are eight ordained associate pastors. Each of their wives is deeply committed to and involved in Vision of the Future, following the example of Marfa Cabrera. Husbands and wives work as pastoral teams. When neither of the Cabreras is there, associate pastors preach and heal.

Believers in each of the forty church locations are cared for by a number of local assistant pastors, deacons, deaconesses, and Christian workers. In the city of Cordoba, for example, between eighty and ninety volunteer workers give many hours on a weekly basis to ministry in the area of their spiritual gifts. Some are teachers, some open their homes for home cell groups, some pray for the sick at home or in the hospital, some take care of administrative matters, some set up or take down furniture for the meetings, some are counselors, some are intercessors, some evangelize.

Not only is Omar Cabrera's ministry different from that of traditional crusade evangelists because he assumes responsibility for pastoral care, but it also is different from that of traditional *churches*. The traditional church asks believers to come to the preacher on a regular basis. Vision of the Future sends preachers to believers. It is a centrifugal church.

Not every pastor could travel 7,000 miles a month to visit parishioners as Cabrera does, so I do not expect he will have many imitators. But his is the best example I have yet seen of combining crusade evangelism methodology with church growth. Vision of the Future has grown from 30,000 in 1979 to 145,000 today, a decadal rate of over 2,000 percent!

The second way Omar Cabrera differs from many traditional crusade evangelists is that he ministers in supernatural power. In the tradition of Matthew 10:7-8, he not only preaches the gospel of the kingdom but heals the sick, cleanses the lepers, raises the dead, and casts out demons. He operates in power evangelism on a daily basis.

Cabrera takes seriously the demonic hierarchy which Satan has given jurisdiction over a geographical area. Before opening a new location for his church, he breaks the grip of the principalities and powers which have been assigned the territory. To do this, he shuts himself up alone in a hotel room in the city for a minimum of four or five days of prayer and fasting. Even Marfa is not allowed in the room unless specifically called. There he enters into spiritual warfare and remains until, in the power of the Holy Spirit, the enemy is defeated. Because this happens, people often will be saved and healed in Cabrera's meetings before he starts preaching.

My wife Doris and I recently had the privilege of traveling several thousand miles with the Cabreras and attending a number of their meetings. Each began with public prayer renouncing all the demons or evil spirits in the auditorium and casting them out in the name of Jesus. The resulting presence of the Holy Spirit was awesome.

God gives Cabrera words of knowledge for certain illnesses on certain nights. On one night, for example, it was for hernia. Scores of people went forward. Cabrera does not lay on hands individually, but prays for all at once. Many, however, are healed before he prays, and some are invited to the platform to give testimony. That night three women were healed of hernias they had for thirty, thiry-two, and forty years. Another had been scheduled for surgery that week, but her hernia disappeared. She looked as though she had won the Argentine lottery!

The same night, after he had started his sermon, Cabrera stopped, pointed to a woman in her fifties with a bandage on her left leg, and said, "Stand up."

She did.

"What's wrong with your leg?" he asked.

"A bleeding tropical ulcer," she replied.

"Come up here and take off the bandage. God has healed you!"

She obeyed and the sore was completely closed and dry.

Such public displays of God's power are as effective for evangelism today as they were in the Book of Acts. As I have said many times, supernatural power for healing the sick and casting out demons is not a prerequisite for bringing lost people to Jesus Christ. But when it is present it helps a lot! I believe we are going to see much more power evangelism even here in the United States in these closing years of the twentieth century.

EIGHT

God's Gifts Revived

A S WE PREACH THE GOSPEL to all nations, ministering with signs and wonders, God gives gifts of many kinds. Healing and deliverance, we have seen, are no longer the property of Pentecostals and charismatics alone. Nor are they to be relegated to a distant age in the past. But other gifts are being revived as well and shared out among many Christians. I want to share with you a few examples of how God has richly blessed the work of evangelism with miraculous gifts.

The Gift of Language

On the day of Pentecost the believers, "filled with the Holy Spirit," went out of the upper room and into the streets of Jerusalem "speaking in other tongues as the Spirit gave them utterance" (Acts 2:4). The people who heard them were amazed because those motley Galileans, who undoubtedly were monolingual Aramaic speakers (with perhaps some knowledge of Greek as a trade language), communicated in such a way that the people heard "each in our own language" (Acts 2:8).

By count they had come from sixteen different places, so presumably the disciples were using, for evangelistic purposes, at least sixteen foreign languages they had never learned.

So far as the record indicates, this was the first miracle God did through the disciples after Jesus left the earth. It is remarkable because there is no indication in the Gospels that during the time Jesus was training his followers such a thing had ever occurred. Nor do we see Jesus himself using languages he had never learned.

It could well be that this miraculous work of the Holy Spirit was accomplishing two things. It obviously was directing the gospel to unbelievers in their heart language. At the same time it may have been sending a message to the disciples that Jesus' promises were true. Jesus had said that "He who believes in me, the works that I do he will do also; and greater works than these he will do, because I go to my Father" (Jn 14:12).

Was the Holy Spirit sending us a message also? Could it be that the gospel is communicated today in languages which those who preach the message have never learned?

Some months ago I met a remarkable missionary couple named James and Jaime Thomas. Soon after they were married a few years ago, they went to Argentina under Maranatha Ministries.

Neither James nor Jaime had learned any Spanish while growing up in Kentucky. James had enrolled in a Spanish course in high school, but dropped it because he was doing poorly and didn't want to lower his grade point average. When he arrived in Cordoba, Argentina, he began planting a church by using an interpreter. God blessed, and a small church was soon under way.

At this point, James invited a Puerto Rican Pentecostal evangelist, Ben Soto, to speak in the evening service at their small church. About 150 people were present. Soto was preaching fervently in Spanish, but suddenly stopped.

The silence startled the congregation. They thought something had happened to the preacher. But he was all right. He said, in English, "James and Jaime, God has just told me he is going to give you the gift of Spanish." He invited them up front, laid on hands, and blessed what God was doing.

Then he said, "James, take over."

James hardly knew what to do because he hadn't felt anything during the prayer. So he called for his interpreter. But Soto insisted that James do it on his own in Spanish.

James reluctantly picked up the announcements, written in English, and began, "*En ... esta ... semana ... vamos ... a. ...*" and broke into fluent, Argentine-accented Spanish. From that moment on he has spoken it like a native and written it with correct grammar, spelling, and accent marks.

Not only that, but when God recently called James from Argentina to Guatemala, he found himself switching to a Guatemalan accent. He demonstrated to me (I am fluent in Spanish) how he could speak the dialects of Honduras, Venezuela and Mexico as well as Argentina and Guatemala. Very few native Spanish speakers can do that.

Meanwhile Jaime had learned even less Spanish than James. She was so terrified when facing someone with whom she could not communicate, that she would not even answer a knock on the door. But at the end of this church service led by Soto, some women began to ask her questions in Spanish. She understood, and answered in Spanish. She has been speaking it ever since.

In order to minister in Bolivia, my wife and I had to learn Spanish by living with Bolivians and studying from books. The Thomases are the only people I personally know who have received a gift of language. I have heard vague references about some, and I have read about two other cases. One was reported by Jon and Cher Cadd who fly for Mission Aviation Fellowship in Zimbabwe. On one occasion they flew Pastor Jerry Rozelle and an African interpreter named Patrick to the northern area of Kanyamba where they located the Vidoma people for the first time.

However, the Vidoma spoke a language Patrick had never heard and could not understand. Discouraged, they prayed. God answered by giving Patrick the Vidoma language. Patrick was so surprised he acted as if he had seen a lion! They preached and 120 gave their lives to the Lord.

The other case is told by Bruce Olson, missionary to Colombia, in his book *Bruchko* (Creation House). Olson had evangelized the Motilone Indians, a fierce, isolated jungle tribe. They had never had contact with neighboring tribes, but God called a group of them to evangelize the Yukos. At that time they did not realize that other languages besides Motilone even existed. But they stayed with the Yukos for several weeks and communicated with them naturally, sharing Jesus with those who had never heard. Incidentally, Yuko is not a dialect of Motilone, but an entirely different language.

"I can only conclude that God's Holy Spirit made the Motilones speak and understand Yuko," Olson says.

Whether Patrick in Zimbabwe or the Motilones in Colombia spoke the other languages from then on, as did James and Jaime Thomas, I do not know. But I am learning that God does work in very surprising ways to see that the gospel is made known.

Stories like this highlight God's power and bring glory to him. But they must not lead us to presumption. I would think 99.9 percent of cross-cultural missionaries still will have to learn languages in the normal human way. Our school at Fuller teaches courses on how to learn languages, and we accept this as the rule. But in this, as in all other areas of Christian service, we are open to God's surprises—and we thank him for them when they come.

The Gift of Prophecy

When I went to seminary back in the fifties I was taught that the "prophecy" referred to in the New Testament was a synonym for preaching. I learned that the word meant both "foretelling" and "forthtelling." However, while there was some significant foretelling of the future recorded in the Bible, we were not to expect that in the present age. The New Testament canon had been closed and in it God had said just about all he wanted to say to the human race. Our task was to study the Scriptures and apply what we find there to contemporary life situations. This was my first understanding of prophecy today.

I accepted this teaching and went to the mission field to serve the Lord. Sometime during those next sixteen years in Bolivia my understanding of prophecy began to change. Some people I respected believed that God had not said all he wanted to say in the first century, but that he was still communicating directly with believers in the twentieth century.

In the later seventies I wrote *Your Spiritual Gifts Can Help Your Church Grow* (Regal Books). When I began the project, I put myself on the spot by resolving that I would write a succinct definition for each of the twenty-seven gifts I had identified. No other author I know of had previously done that. The definitions were relatively easy for many of the gifts, but prophecy was not one of those. I clearly recall the struggle I had to go through to admit to myself that I no longer held that prophecy was preaching and nothing else. Here is the definition of prophecy I wrote:

> *The gift of prophecy is the special ability that God gives to certain members of the body of Christ to receive and communicate an immediate message of God to His people through a divinely anointed utterance.*

When I published the book I wondered if that definition would come in for criticism. To date over 100,000 copies have circulated and, much to my surprise, I have heard virtually no negative reaction. This leads me to believe that the Christian public is much more open to understanding prophecy as a form of present-day revelation from God than they were when I went to seminary.

Scripture is infallible; prophets today are not. This is why some safeguards are needed. Three principal checkpoints should be used whenever prophecy is being given.

1. *Recognition of the gift of prophecy.* Some members of the body of Christ have the gift of prophecy as I defined it above. On a somewhat regular basis they are being used to transmit God's message.

I like the way British theologian Michael Green describes what happens: "The Spirit has taken over and addresses the hearers through [the prophet]."

2. *Agreement with Scripture.* No disagreement with Scripture is allowed in a true prophecy. Checking a prophecy against the written Word of God is essential, because God will not contradict himself.

3. *Confirmation from other members of the body of Christ.* One of the strongest safeguards against false prophecy is the agreement of other Christians.

I myself do not have the gift of prophecy. I have never received a full-blown prophecy as many others have. On several occasions, however, I have had God speak directly to me through prophecies of other brothers and sisters.

So far as I can recall, the first time it happened to me was in November 1983. God wanted to make sure I got the message, because he gave it to me five times in that one month through five different people. All of the prophecies had to do with God's purpose in calling me out to be one of the leaders in the movement I now call the "Third Wave." Even though I was inexperienced I had no doubt in my spirit on any of the five occasions that God was speaking to me directly.

The first prophecy came from a woman from my Sunday school class in a prayer meeting in our own home. The message lasted for several minutes and declared that God had anointed me for a new work. The second came from a man in my Sunday school class who knew nothing about the first one. He wrote it down for me, and I have a copy. The third was one of my seminary students, a missionary from Japan, who gave it to me after class. The fourth was a telephone call from a woman who used to work in our office. I had not seen or spoken to her in years. But the word was crystal clear. The fifth came from a pastor attending one of my church planting seminars. I took notes as he spoke, but I have not seen him since nor do I recall his name.

God is a real person; he loves us and he wants us to know it—and it should not surprise us if he chooses to speak directly to us from time to time.

Raising the Dead

One day as I was carrying on a discussion with a respected Christian theologian on healing, miracles, and the supernatural in general, we found ourselves in agreement on many issues. Then somehow the subject of raising the dead came up. Immediately our dialogue took a turn for the worse.

In a somewhat irritated tone, my friend said, "There—that is where I draw the line! Healing, yes. Casting out demons, perhaps. I'm willing to talk about those things, but not raising the dead. That is an extremism which I cannot tolerate."

My friend is a Bible-believing Christian. He recognizes the fact that when Jesus sent out the twelve disciples he commanded them to "heal the sick, cleanse the lepers, raise the dead, cast out demons" (Mt 10:8). He believes that Jesus raised Lazarus from the dead, that Peter raised Dorcas, and that Paul raised Eutychus. He does not hold, as some do, that the "sign gifts" went out with the apostolic age. But something in his mind will not allow him even to consider possible evidence that dead people might be raised today.

I often wish I were a psychologist who could analyze the thought processes which produce such an intellectual blockage. But the explanation may be as simple as understanding the attitude of a doubting Thomas. Thomas refused to believe that Jesus had been raised from the dead until he saw and touched the wounds in his hands and side.

Perhaps my friend can accept supernatural healing because he has seen it, but not raising the dead because he hasn't seen it as yet. Jesus didn't scold doubting Thomas. He said, "Thomas, because you have seen me, you have believed." But then he went on, "Blessed are those who have not seen and yet have believed" (Jn 20:29).

The materialistically oriented scientific worldview of most Americans, Christian and non-Christian, requires them to be somewhat skeptical. Believing reports of something as unusual as raising the dead could possibly label them as naive or even gullible.

Several months ago I was talking about these things with another theologian. He asserted rather categorically that dead persons are not raised. Death to him was irreversible. When I mentioned reports from the mission fields, he said, "Yes, it always happens out there someplace where you can't check it." Then I asked him whether he would believe it if it happened here in the United States in a hospital not five miles from where we were standing.

I was referring to an incident, reported in *Christian Life* (September 1983), which involved the swimming pool accident of a year-old boy, John Eric Cadenhead. I was personally involved only to the extent that the boy's mother attended my church and that the two pediatricians who treated him also were members of our church. The boy was declared legally dead by the paramedics and had been without vital signs for a minimum of forty minutes, probably longer. Medication had caused some electrical activity of the heart muscles after he got to the hospital; but there still were no vital signs. Through prayer, the baby later revived and suffered no brain damage.

So the question becomes, was the baby dead or not? Most people with a Western worldview would say, "Of course not. The fact the boy now is alive proves he could not ever have been dead." Interestingly enough, however, the nurses in the hospital nicknamed John Eric "baby Lazarus," and the secular press, the *Pasadena Star*

News, ran a front-page feature article on him under the headline, "Miracle."

About two-thirds of the world today would not question the possibility of a dead person returning to life. Their worldview seems nearer to that of the people to whom Jesus, Peter, and Paul ministered in New Testament times. When Jairus' daughter was raised, we have no record of anyone saying, "Well, the fact that she's alive proves she never died after all."

In recent years, when I have traveled to the Third World, I have asked leaders there if they know of the dead being raised. In Brazil I heard three direct accounts of such incidents. I talked to a Nazarene pastor who himself had been raised from the dead when he was two years old. I interviewed a pastor's wife in Argentina who was under water for thirty minutes and who described in detail her experience "out of the body." I have heard of similar stories in the Philippines, Indonesia, and India. Case studies of raising the dead have been coming out of China for some time.

A fascinating interview appeared in the Summer 1985 issue of *Church Growth Digest,* published by the British Church Growth Association. Editor Monica Hill interviewed Bishop Benson Idahosa of Benin City, Nigeria. Idahosa pastors a church of over 10,000 and has recently dedicated a new sanctuary which seats 20,000.

"We have heard that you have seen many amazing miracles and that you have even seen the dead raised. Is this true?" Monica Hill asked.

I love the nonchalance of Idahosa's response: "Well,

my calling is not to raise the dead, but I have seen it seven times. One is my wife's niece who has five children now. She was the first I saw twenty-three years ago and since that time I have seen six others. But I don't go around saying that, because that is not my call. My call is to preach Christ."

I, too, now believe that dead people are literally being raised in the world today. As soon as I say that, some ask if I believe it is "normative." I doubt if it would be normative in any local situation, but it probably is normative in terms of the universal body of Christ. Even though it is an extremely uncommon event, I would not be surprised if it were happening several times a year.

One of my objectives in bringing up the matter in this chapter is to open channels of communication. In some circles the subject is taboo. One missionary (in a foreign country) said he would tell me of a case of a dead person being raised if I promised I would not let his supporting constituency know about it. I don't see that attitude in the Bible.

Why does God raise some dead people on certain occasions? I believe it is to open the doors to what happened when Peter raised Dorcas: "It became known throughout all Joppa, and many believed in the Lord" (Acts 9:42).

God's central purpose is to seek and save the lost, and at times he does it with unusually great manifestations of power.

NINE

A Deeper Walk

FOCUSING ON THE SPECTACULAR MIRACLES that God is doing today to make his name and power known can sometimes lead to a false impression. We might be tempted to think that signs and wonders are an end in themselves. Jesus warned his disciples against this error. When they returned from their preaching mission, where they had won great victories over demons in Jesus' name, he told them, "Do not rejoice in this, that the spirits are subject to you; but rejoice that your names are written in heaven" (Lk 10:20).

In our walk with Jesus, there's always more. He is always leading us to come further with him in ministry, in suffering, and in the spiritual life of his body. Some people accuse Christians of looking at the world through "rose-colored glasses"—especially those who emphasize God's power to heal and to deliver. "You're ignoring the real problems," they say. Others say, "Sure, you can accept Christ with joy when things go well. But can you endure to the end through difficulties? Are you bearing fruit that will last?" I agree with these concerns, and I want to close by pointing us toward a deeper walk with Jesus—not away from the miraculous, but toward the Miracle Worker.

Three Kinds of Death

"Holistic ministry" is being emphasized in Christian circles these days. I, too, believe we must minister to the whole person—body, soul, and spirit. We should be feeding stomachs as well as saving souls. Jesus not only preached the gospel of the kingdom, he demonstrated it by healing the sick. He expects us to do likewise.

Some theologians explain this in terms of the "evangelistic mandate" and the "cultural mandate." The mission of the church includes both evangelizing and addressing social and material problems. The Third Wave, with its emphasis on supernatural signs and wonders, buys into this holistic mission.

Having affirmed this, an important question lingers. Is there any priority? Yes, there is. While both mandates must be explicitly obeyed, the evangelistic mandate is primary. The biblical reasons for this go back to the Garden of Eden.

God told Adam and Eve they could eat from all the trees except one. If they ate from the tree of the knowledge of good and evil they would die (Gn 2:17). Satan tempted them. They ate the forbidden fruit. And they died. Adam and Eve did not drop over on the spot like Ananias and Sapphira, however, so in what sense did they die? They died in three senses: spiritually, physically, and materially (or socially). Let's look at these in reverse order.

Material or social death. In the Garden of Eden, all of Adam and Eve's material needs were met with little or no effort. Sin put an end to that. They were driven from the garden, and God cursed the ground. Thorns and thistles began to grow. This was the beginning of the myriad of human problems experienced through the years: poverty, war, oppression, discrimination, slavery, social injustice, famine.

How long will these problems last? They will be with us until Jesus returns and establishes the New Jerusalem. God sent cherubim to keep Adam and Eve from having access to the Garden of Eden and the tree of life. But the tree of life will be there once again in the New Jerusalem (Rv 22:2).

Meanwhile, as Jesus said, the poor will be with us. Material or social death is a constant reminder of Satan's presence and activity. So what do we, as Christians, do about it? We fulfill the cultural mandate. We love our neighbor as ourselves, as Jesus instructed us. We follow Jesus' example when he said, "The Spirit of the Lord is upon me because he has anointed me to preach the gospel to the poor" (Lk 4:18).

Physical death. Before the fall, sickness and death were not a part of the Garden of Eden. When Adam and Eve sinned, the immediate result was that they became mortal. Physical death became inevitable, and, of course, they both eventually expired. It was a direct result of the efforts of Satan.

In the New Jerusalem there will be no more death, sorrow, crying, or pain (Rv 21:4). Meanwhile, we live in a world where sickness, pain, and physical death are constant reminders of Satan's presence and influence. What do we, as Christians, do about it?

Again, we fulfill the cultural mandate. We do the best we can to alleviate these areas of human suffering. We train surgeons, encourage medical research, produce therapeutic drugs, and build hospitals. We also draw on supernatural resources which God has promised us.

Jesus expects his disciples in every nation to continue doing whatever he commanded the first disciples to do (Mt 28:20). The first time he sent them out, he commanded them to preach saying, "The kingdom of heaven is at hand." To back up those words, he commanded them to "heal the sick, cleanse the lepers, raise the dead, cast out demons" (Mt 10:7, 8). This is the reason we, today, in obedience to the cultural mandate, attempt to do what Jesus told us to do. This is one of the major distinctives of the Third Wave.

Spiritual death. Spiritual death is the most serious of the three types of death. It is the separation of human beings from God. God created Adam and Eve to have fellowship with him, but sin broke that fellowship, much to the delight of Satan.

Why do I say it's the most serious of all?

Notice that material and social problems are temporal; so are their solutions. We can feed the starving in Ethiopia. We can eradicate apartheid. We can sign international peace treaties. And we should. It is part of our Christian duty. But the problems will keep coming back until we get to the New Jerusalem.

The same thing applies to ministry in the supernatural. We can heal the sick. We can perform signs and wonders in Jesus' name. But none of those things is permanent. Everyone whom Jesus healed eventually died. Even Lazarus, whom Jesus raised from the dead, later died.

In contrast, the solution for spiritual death is not temporal but eternal. When a lost person is born again, follows Jesus Christ, and reestablishes fellowship with the Father, it lasts forever. The Bible calls it *eternal* life.

Bringing this about is fulfilling the evangelistic mandate. It is what Jesus came and died for: "The Son of man has come to seek and to save that which was lost" (Lk 19:10). Sharing the gospel with lost men and women is our highest calling in doing the work of God here on earth.

So, is there a priority? Of course. We need to obey the cultural mandate. We need to help solve social problems. We need to heal the sick and cast out demons. But even more important is the evangelistic mandate.

Death began in the Garden of Eden. It will end in the New Jerusalem. Our major concern must be that when the Lamb opens the gates to the New Jerusalem the maximum number of people will be there to say, "Amen! Blessing and glory and wisdom, thanksgiving and honor and power and might, be to our God forever and ever" (Rv 7:12).

Power and the Poor

Ministry to the poor, however, is not separate from our evangelistic mandate, even from evangelism through signs and wonders. The Bible tells us that God loves all people, but that he is especially concerned for the poor. Jesus has given us the authority to overcome Satan, even to deal with the social problems he has caused. I have seen God's power at work in this way in my own church.

Every New Year's day, Pasadena, California, where I live, is featured on national television with the Tournament of Roses parade and the Rose Bowl game. Those who watch it do not see pictures of poverty. However large numbers of people in Pasadena, as in most other American cities, are poor. There is a large minority population here which rapidly is becoming the majority. The heaviest concentration of poor live in the predominately black Northwest Pasadena area.

Buying drugs in Northwest Pasadena is almost as easy as buying groceries. Drug pushers offer curbside service. Prostitutes openly ply their trade on the streets. Gang fights and the accompanying violence are daily occurrences. The area is rated by California law enforcement personnel as having the highest daytime crime rate in the state. The Pasadena Police Department does what it can, but even the police chief admits it cannot solve all the problems there.

While Northwest Pasadena would repel many Christian workers, it became an attraction to one well-respected leader, John Perkins. Perkins, founder of the famous Voice of Calvary ministries in Mississippi, moved to Pasadena with his wife Vera Mae in 1982 to begin a new chapter in his ministry.

Readers of Perkins' outstanding books, *Let Justice Roll Down* and *With Justice for All,* know that his threefold strategy for ministering to the poor is relocation, reconciliation, and redistribution. For Perkins, the relocation meant moving into Northwest Pasadena. The house he bought was in the vortex of one of the top two drug-dealing neighborhoods, next door to a house openly recognized as a drug supermarket.

The challenge is formidable and quite different from Mississippi's. For one thing, opposition to Perkins in Mississippi was racially motivated and came from the white community. But in Pasadena it is reversed. The white community is on Perkins's side, and the attacks are coming from blacks. How is this going to be dealt with?

Perkins is a skilled social activist and community developer, one of America's best. But he realizes he is up against more than just social problems. He is battling principalities and powers. Spiritual warfare is needed.

What all this implies, Perkins does not yet know. I feel very much a part of his experience because soon after coming to Pasadena, God led him to become a member of my Sunday School class, the 120 Fellowship of Lake Avenue Congregational Church.

He has been a tremendous blessing to the class because he has shown us how we can minister to the poor in a practical way. Some members of the class have been recruited to become part of Perkins's staff in what is called the Harambee Center.

As a class, we are allowing God to show us his supernatural power and how to apply it in places like Northwest Pasadena. Much of God's teaching comes through experience.

A notable experience surprised John Perkins in

November 1983. One of our class prayer team, Cathryn Hoellwarth, had a word of knowledge that God wanted to minister to someone who had a painful digestive disorder. She had a clear picture of it, but no one in class responded. So Cathryn prayed about it that week. On Thursday, God told her specifically that it was John Perkins. He had not been in class that morning.

The next Sunday he was there. Cathryn approached him. She asked if he had stomach problems, then began to describe his symptoms with pinpoint accuracy. Perkins said he had been suffering for months, that it was getting worse, and that this particular Sunday was his worst day yet. So Cathryn invited him to come to the prayer room after class.

Perkins, like many of us evangelicals, had little background to prepare him for something like this, so he was hesitant. He asked my wife Doris and me if we would go to the prayer room with him, and we did. Tremendous power was evident, and we felt he had been healed.

We could not be sure, however, because just then Perkins was named to President Reagan's special Commission on Hunger and had to spend several weeks traveling in other parts of the country. But when he returned in January he stood up in class and gave his testimony.

"I'm not an emotional man," he said (with some emotion), "but last November when the prayer team prayed for me after class, something happened. I now feel better than I have in years. Praise the Lord!"

Here was a direct touch of God's power. Through it,

God undoubtedly was sending a message. What the message is we do not exactly know, but we think it may have something to do with spiritual warfare in Northwest Pasadena and God's plan to break the demonic powers over some of the neighborhoods there.

Many people, more familiar with this than we are, tell us that Satan assigns sophisticated, high-ranking princes of the demons jurisdiction over selected geographical territories. In some, the kingdom of evil is so well entrenched that any approach by the kingdom of God is resisted violently.

This could well be, because a short time ago John Perkins' home, the Harambee Center, was attacked and the windows broken by bricks. A week later it was bombed with a Molotov cocktail and a homemade firebomb. Fortunately, no serious damage was done.

Perkins responds to the violence with Christian love.

"These young people don't see themselves as criminals, but as business people who have a right to control their community," he says. He admits they probably regard him and his work as obstacles to their way of life, and are taking the kind of action they consider appropriate.

But not even the law-abiding neighbors came out in support of John and Vera Mae, even after the bombing. Why? They are thoroughly intimidated by the criminal element.

Perkins recently wrote me a note. "We need prayer— and supernatural power—that the power of Satan might be broken in this community," he said. We already are seeing some signs of victory.

I do not believe that God wants people poor. The

kingdom of God is a realm of justice, not inequality, discrimination, and oppression. But how to see the values of the kingdom displayed in Northwest Pasadena is our immediate concern.

None of the "isms" (such as capitalism, communism, or socialism) have seemed to bring justice to the poor. Welfare and food stamps often have only intensified the problem. There must be another way—and that way may well begin by taking the principalities and powers seriously.

One of the lines being explored in the Third Wave is the role of supernatural power in dealing with social injustice, and I have a high degree of confidence that in God's time we will begin to see some concrete answers.

When Suffering Comes

Another effect of Satan's victory in the Garden of Eden is suffering. It's not only the suffering of the poor—it's our own suffering, right in our own churches. Just let me ask you: Have you noticed that when a church develops a strong healing ministry the number of people in wheelchairs and on crutches who attend seems to multiply?

Not only is this a common phenomenon, but it is almost equally common for these folk to keep coming despite having received prayer for healing on a regular basis with no noticeable improvement in their condition.

This observation raises a number of issues constantly faced by those who have a ministry of praying for the sick. For one thing, we realize that we who pray for the sick do not do the healing. Only God heals. Sometimes he chooses to heal, sometimes he does not. Sometimes he heals instantly, sometimes he heals gradually. Sometimes he heals directly, sometimes he uses other means such as surgeons.

Recognizing this helps us see praying for the sick as a win-win situation. If God heals immediately we obviously have won, and we praise the Lord. But even when he does not we also have won because we are reflecting the compassion and the love of the Father for those for whom we pray, and almost invariably they recognize it. They thank us for the prayer and go on trusting God even though their suffering may continue. And they come back for more prayer.

We read in the Gospels that when sick people came to Jesus, he healed them all. We wish we could do the same. But failure helps us realize we are but vessels of clay and not yet completely like our Savior. Jesus was absolutely sinless and we only strive for that goal, fully realizing that in this life we will continue to fall short.

I recently did a good bit of thinking on the meaning of suffering when a close friend of mine, Tom Brewster, died in the operating room. Tom and his wife, Betty Sue, were members of my Sunday School class, the 120 Fellowship. Furthermore, the two of them, both with earned Ph.D.s, taught with me on the faculty of the School of World Mission at Fuller Seminary. Tom had suffered a diving accident at eighteen and for almost thirty years was a paraplegic. This did not deter him from becoming a ranking world expert in language-culture learning. He boasted good-naturedly that his wheelchair probably had been to more countries than any other wheelchair on earth.

I observed Tom Brewster at very close range for many years. Not a day went by that he did not suffer. Nevertheless, I saw that while he suffered, even in this life he had mentally conquered suffering and had risen above it.

"I shudder to think what my life would have been if I hadn't had the accident," he said. He recognized the benefits God brought through the suffering, never blaming God for either his accident or his handicap. He knew that while the sovereign God permitted the accident, he did not cause it.

Tom constantly exhibited the fruit of the Spirit. He could have become angry, bitter, or rebellious over his condition, but he did not. He lived with a positive attitude.

In recent years Tom joined others of us in the Third Wave and engaged in spiritual warfare. He allowed the power of God to be channeled through him, and he frequently prayed for the healing of others who were not suffering nearly as much as he. Tom rejoiced when they were healed even though he wasn't.

Through it all, he never lost hope. At one point he wrote a "Declaration of Expectation" and distributed it to his circle of friends. In it he affirmed his belief in God's desire to heal and shared a feeling that God's healing power would be applied to him, but throughout he upheld a firm confidence in God's sovereignty.

Whether he ever walked in this life or not, Tom's God was still King of kings and Lord of lords.

He never did walk. Emergency bladder surgery could not correct years of degeneration and he went to be with the Lord. He, of course, is walking now. Meanwhile, what have we learned about suffering?

1. Suffering is real. I see no merit in those approaches which attempt to deny the validity of suffering. Nor do I believe the reason we suffer is that we do not have enough faith to deny it. I once saw a deacon point to a church member in a wheelchair and say, "Sister, when you have enough faith, you'll be up off that chair." Peter and John did not say that to the lame man at the temple gate.

2. Most biblical references to suffering attribute it to persecution for the faith, not to sickness. Jesus' suffering was at the hands of Jewish and Roman enemies of the gospel. So far as we know he was never sick.

3. God is not the cause of suffering. God is a God of love. Jesus never inflicted suffering on his disciples or friends. As the catechism says, "Man's chief end is to glorify God and enjoy Him forever." Suffering is, by definition, unenjoyable. Adam and Eve were not created to suffer, but suffering came to them through Satan's temptation and their fall into sin. While God promises freedom from suffering in the New Jerusalem, he permits the enemy to cause it in the here and now. Two of the chief biblical examples of suffering—Job, and Paul's thorn in the flesh—are attributed directly to Satan. Why God permits it is a great mystery which

theologians have been trying to fathom for centuries. To be honest, we simply don't know.

4. We do not accept suffering passively. We live in a period characterized by a clash of the kingdom of darkness against the kingdom of light. We engage in spiritual warfare because we wrestle against principalities and powers and spiritual wickedness in high places. We pray for those who are sick, demonized, oppressed, poor, or emotionally unbalanced, calling down God's power against the enemy.

5. Meanwhile, we expect God to teach us through suffering. For reasons only he knows, God does not choose to relieve all the suffering we pray against. In those cases we refuse to allow the enemy to defeat us.

6. In all we glorify God. He is King of kings and Lord of lords. We love him and trust him. We recognize the fact that we see "in a mirror dimly." We know in part and prophesy in part. Suffering does not change God or our loving relationship with him. Prayer, praise, and perseverance in suffering are all part of that relationship, the fruit of which is a deep spiritual life.

Cultivating the Spiritual Life

Most Christians know that part and parcel of the lifestyle of the kingdom is something called spirituality. Many, on New Year's Eve, resolve to be more spiritual the next year. It is commonly accepted that Christians are more spiritual than atheists, and that some Christians are more spiritual than others.

But with all these assumptions about spirituality, few

of us take the time and effort to think through just what we mean by it. And when we do, we find that not all believers agree. I recently took part in a symposium where six different Christian leaders addressed the meaning of spirituality. I was surprised to find how divergent their opinions were, although that divergence should have been somewhat predictable since the leaders came from different denominational backgrounds. Afterward, I found myself feeling that probably none of them was "wrong," but that each, in his or her way, was right.

The Bible says that "we see in a mirror dimly," meaning that none of us has a corner on truth. Only when we leave this life and arrive in heaven will we see "face to face." Meanwhile, we learn from each other as each brings his or her own perspective.

My perspective is that of a person dedicated primarily to world evangelization. So far I have spent the first half of my adult ministry as a missionary; the second half as a professor of missions. When I look at the Christian life in general, or spirituality in particular, I focus on the harvest. Part of my praying is to the Lord of the harvest, that he will send forth laborers into the harvest field. Fruit is very important to me, so I tend to connect spirituality to fruit.

One of the places the Bible speaks of fruit is John 15:16—"You did not choose me, but I chose you and appointed you that you should go and bear fruit, and that your fruit should remain." Bearing fruit, then, is an important aspect of our ongoing relationship to Jesus.

How are we to bear this fruit? Earlier in the same

chapter Jesus says, "I am the vine, you are the branches. He who abides in me, and I in him, bears much fruit; for without me you can do nothing" (Jn 15:5).

Here Jesus is talking about grape farming. As everyone who has seen this knows, grapes grow on branches; none grow on vinestocks. Apparently, then, Jesus is telling us that he himself is not intending to bear fruit here on earth. All the fruit bearing is left to us, the branches. But not all branches bear fruit. If a branch is separated from the vine, it cannot bear fruit. Why? Because it has no power to bear fruit in and of itself. The power is in the vine. The branch is simply a channel for that power.

To me, Jesus' vine-and-branch analogy is a profound key to understanding spirituality. Fruitful Christians are locked into Jesus as the branch is locked into the vine. No relationship could be more intimate than the branch and the vine. But this is what Jesus asks and expects of all of us. Intimacy and all that it implies gets right to the heart of spirituality. The more intimate our relationship to God (Father, Son, and Holy Spirit), the more spiritual we become.

I believe we need to cultivate intimacy with God on two important levels: the personal and corporate. And we need to do both simultaneously.

On the personal level, I see a daily time alone with God as indispensable for intimacy. I was taught this when I first became a Christian thirty-five years ago and practiced it. But it eventually became boring and I stopped the practice for a time. More recently, however, since becoming involved in the Third Wave, I have taken it up again. Now it is anything but boring.

What made the difference?

In the early years I knew very little about intimacy with the Father. I focused mostly on Bible study and not enough on a personal relationship with God. Now I know more about worship, reverence, and praise. I seek a daily refilling of the Holy Spirit in a way I can actually feel his presence. Jesus said about the good shepherd that "the sheep hear his voice." I am beginning to distinguish the voice of God from my own thoughts and to allow him to speak to me directly.

I still study the Bible, of course, but I find this other dimension of personal intimacy equally important. Then I ask God to give me the ability to obey both the Scriptures and his direct word to me. Intimacy without obedience, like faith without works, is dead.

The amount of time one spends in this is more important than some people realize. While I do not think time spent alone with God always is directly proportional to one's spirituality, I do believe there is some relationship. I cannot tell my wife I love her, then not spend much time with her. The same thing applies to God. Most of us, I feel, would become more spiritual if we spent more time with God.

On the corporate level, all of us need to establish a primary relationship to a segment of the body of Christ. For some, it is their congregation; for others, it is a small support group. Whatever form it takes, the group needs to cultivate intimacy with God.

My primary group is my adult Sunday School class. I depend a great deal on that group for my spirituality. For example, members of the class have the spiritual gift of intercession, and they pray for me. As a result, I believe the quality of my ministry has improved.

What are other results of this kind of spirituality? Like the branch, we become channels. The power of God now can flow through us. We have power to grow in grace, to exhibit the fruit of the Spirit, to live a holy life. We have power for witnessing. We become useful instruments in God's hands for spreading his kingdom throughout the earth.

We also have power for ministry. We are able to reflect the values of the kingdom of God in our lives. We live a kingdom lifestyle. We preach the good news to the poor. We take action to liberate the oppressed. We feed the hungry. We heal the sick, cleanse the lepers, raise the dead, and cast out demons.

Only if we are branches in the vine can we move effectively in the flow of the Holy Spirit in the Third Wave. Then we will be able to fulfill God's desire for our lives: that we bear fruit and fruit that remains.

Index

Other Books of Interest from Servant Books

Knowing the Truth about the Resurrection
Our Response to the Empty Tomb
William L. Craig

Examining the evidence for the burial of Jesus, the empty tomb, the resurrection appearances, and the beginning of Christianity, William Craig demonstrates why the resurrection is the only answer that fits the facts. He answers important questions like: Did Jesus rise from the dead? Is there evidence for the historical resurrection? Can we trust the resurrection account in the Gospel? What does the resurrection mean for us? *$8.95*

Knowing the Truth about Heaven and Hell
Our Choices and Where They Lead Us
Harry Blamires

The choices we make in life really do matter. Here is clear Christian reasoning answering questions such as: How can a loving God punish people? Is hell necessary? Is it possible to reject God's offer of salvation? What will heaven be like? How can we set our hearts on heaven in this life? *$8.95*